1972.

Merry Xmas, Linda & Bill.
May this evoke many happy
memories.

Love,

Uncle Warren & Auntie May.

ANTIQUITIES IN PERIL

ANTIQUITIES IN PERIL

Trevor L. Christie

J. B. Lippincott Company

PHILADELPHIA *and* NEW YORK

For the photographs on the following pages the author gratefully credits:

The British Travel Association: 27, 28, 31
The French Government Tourist Office: 13, 15, 16, 21, 55, 57, 58, 61, 63, 65
Prof. Pietro Gazzola: 34, 36 (bottom), 37, 42
The Greek National Tourist Office: 18, 69, 73, 75
The Italian Government Travel Office: 41
The Italian State Tourist Office: 17, 36 (top), 45, 48, 51
The Japan National Tourist Organization: 118, 119
The Jordan Tourist Information Office: 85, 89, 91
The Library of Congress Photo Service: 137, 138, 140
New York University: 78, 79, 80, 82
The Pakistan Mission to the United Nations: 100, 102, 103
The Soviet Intourist Organization: 124, 125, 126, 128, 130, 131, 133
UNESCO: 19, 39, 44, 70, 71, 96, 108, 109, 110, 111, 114

To My Daughter Joyce Who Remembers the Parthenon

CONTENTS

ANTIQUITIES IN PERIL

I

OUR

CULTURAL HERITAGE

AND ITS ENEMIES

Down through the ages man has recorded his achievements of the past, his aspirations for the future, and his interpretation of the meaning of life on stone, brick, wood, canvas, or any other material that came to hand. Across the face of the earth he has reared great tombs, temples, churches, theaters, and other monuments as testaments to his belief in immortality. In almost every land he has utilized paints and oils to create masterpieces of art as evidence of his love of beauty, form, and harmony. Taken together these constitute his cultural heritage and his legacy to his descendants.

Almost from the beginning, however, it was obvious that the life of most of these monuments and art objects was limited and that they were under constant attack by their enemies: Time, Nature, and Man himself. Over the centuries this took many forms. Fire, water, and earthquakes have destroyed many an historic site in a blinding flash. Weather—too hot or too cold, too humid or too dry —has slowly crumbled others. Bacteria and parasites have devoured them from within and creeping vegetation has strangled them from without. Man as a warrior has destroyed countless treasures since the first battle was fought thousands of years ago. Man as a vandal has looted the work of his ancestors since the days of ancient Egypt. Man as a builder has leveled uncounted others in modern times with the bulldozer and the wrecking ball in the name of progress. Man as a technologist in the industrial age has doomed still others with air pollution as the most recent peril and perhaps the most deadly of all over a long period.

In spite of this carnage a concerted movement to save humanity's cultural patrimony is hardly more than a hundred years old. France was the first big nation to try to halt the destruction when it set up the *Service des Monuments Historiques* in 1830 to protect its landmarks. Britain followed with its National Trust which now owns about one thousand precious properties. As one of the greatest repositories of historic relics, Italy did not establish its Council of Antiquities and Fine Arts until 1933 but has moved swiftly and sternly since. In the United States, New York State was the first to join the effort in 1850 when it acquired George Washington's Revolutionary Headquarters at Newburgh. A decade later the

Mont-Saint-Michel in France.

first President's home and plantation at Mount Vernon were bought and preserved by a patriotic women's society. The Federal government entered the field in the 1890's by purchasing the Civil War battlefields of Gettysburg, Chickamauga, and Shiloh and taking steps to protect the Indian cliff dwellings and pueblos in the Southwest. The National Trust for Historic Preservation was created in 1949 as a semi-official body with a charter from Congress. The United Nations Educational, Scientific, and Cultural Organization (UNESCO) launched the first international effort in this area in 1959 when it sponsored the campaign to save Abu Simbel and the other temples of Nubia from the floodwaters of the Aswan High Dam. This was so successful that it initiated a worldwide crusade in June, 1964, to preserve all monuments wherever they were threatened.

More than fifty nations on five continents have pledged their cooperation and President Lyndon B. Johnson in accepting for the United States said: "UNESCO's International Campaign for monuments is an outstanding contribution to the preservation of the world's cultural legacy. These tangible reminders of past progress, with their emphasis on lasting values, serve as guideposts to a rational and meaningful future. The United States will participate wholeheartedly in your campaign to develop and improve technical and legal measures for the protection, preservation, and restoration of cultural property, and for the safeguarding of the beauty and character of the landscape." Other organizations coping with the problem are the UNESCO-affiliated International Council of Museums, with headquarters in Paris, the International Centre for the study of the Preservation and Restoration of Cultural Property in Rome, the Conservation Center of the New York University Institute of Fine

Arts in New York City, and the Building Research Centre near London.

As a result of these developments many priceless monuments have been rescued for the enrichment of posterity but many others have been sentenced to slow or rapid death. In London great structures such as Westminster Abbey and the House of Commons have been protected for all time, and stringent controls have been placed over lesser landmarks. In Paris famous buildings like Notre Dame Cathedral, the Louvre, the Hôtel des Invalides, housing Napoleon's tomb, have been preserved inviolate.

The Louvre in Paris before being washed.

The Louvre, after.

In Brussels the fifteenth-century Hôtel de Ville (City Hall) in the mellow old Grand' Place has been renovated over the years. In Rome the Colosseum, the Forum, and other ancient edifices have been saved but in Florence some historic palaces are in danger. In such widely diverse cities as Tokyo, Bangkok, Istanbul, and Buenos Aires protective agencies have been set up and strict laws have been enacted for the same purpose but it is a constant struggle against the forces of industrial and residential expansion.

Elsewhere in the world the picture is downright grim. The entire city of Venice, a veritable jewel-box of antiquities, is slowly sinking into its lagoon on the Adriatic Sea. The Leaning Tower of Pisa threatens to fall down because of faulty construction and poor foundation soil. The extraordinary cave paintings of Lascaux in southwest France were attacked by a strange mold and closed to the public. The buildings of Oxford University are the object of a ten-year restoration program to halt erosion of their stones. The Cathedral of Cologne in Western Germany is under constant repair by teams of architects and masons. St. Stephen's Cathedral in Vienna is suffering from the elements and its 450-foot main spire has long been in metal splints while repairs go on. The cathedrals

*The Island of San Giorgio
as seen from Venice.*

of Strasbourg and Rouen are in slow decay. The incomparable Parthenon atop Athen's Acropolis is chipping off stone by stone and is in danger of collapse. The ruins of Aphrodisias in southwest Turkey have been temporarily rescued from peasant squatters but no one knows for how long. The Church of the Holy Sepulchre in Jordanian Jerusalem is being rebuilt from the ground up to save it from disintegration. The great Palace of Emperor Darius I at Persepolis in Iran (Old Persia) is beset by the erosion of wind and weather. The vast ruins of Mohenjo-Daro in West Pakistan are besieged by salt water seeping into their vitals. The colossal temples of Angkor in far-off

The Parthenon in Athens, Greece.

The Apadane Palace in Persepolis, as seen from the Palace of Emperor Darius I.

A fragment of a column with a bull's head at Persepolis.

Cambodia have been snatched from the clutches of the jungle but the battle is never over. The world's largest statue of Buddha (173 feet high) in the mountains of Afghanistan is imperiled by three thousand tons of rock hanging from above. Cleopatra's Needle, a two-hundred-ton obelisk built for an Egyptian Pharaoh, is being eaten away by air pollution in New York's Central Park. Even the boom of jet planes breaking the sound barrier threatens castles in France and other European countries. These are the most dramatic examples of antiquities in peril but almost every stone or brick monument in the world and many famous paintings are in greater or lesser danger.

In the case of monuments, the experts say that the simplest way of preserving them if they are portable is to move them indoors where a constant environment can be maintained and replace them with copies outdoors. If they are too large for this, the best method is to wash them regularly with water but this is extremely expensive because of the labor involved. Among famous edifices that have been given a bath with a scrub brush in recent years are the Church of the Madeleine and most of the monuments of Paris, St. Paul's Cathedral and the statue of Lord Nelson in London, and the Washington Monument in the United States capital.

Some monuments have deteriorated to such an extent, however, that they are beyond such simple treatment and this has given birth to a new school of conservation and restoration by scientists who are working feverishly to discover the causes and combat the inroads of stone "disease." Their work is still in an experimental stage and

The Church of the Madeleine in Paris, before its recent "bath."

The Church of the Madeleine after being washed.

they have no absolute answers to the problems as yet. But they have gone far enough to identify the blackest villain in their laboratories as the fumes poured into the atmosphere by factory chimneys and automobile exhausts. These fumes contain a high content of sulphur dioxide and other gases and the former dissolves in rain or snow to form sulphuric acid, a deadly corrosive. When this settles on a piece of stone it creates a hard black crust of gypsum which collects soot and dust and this attacks the "skin" of the stone, breaks down its resistance, and leads to slow disintegration. It then becomes an easy prey to the elements.

While air pollution may be the greatest cause of "weathering," the experts also point to other enemies: water circulating within the stones, extreme variations in temperature, and the action of bacteria in forming sulphate "sores" which ultimately lead to the death of the "patient." The quality of the stone used, the way it is handled during construction and even its position in the building—whether or not it is exposed to cleansing rainfall—may have a bearing on its life expectancy.

Dr. Seymour Z. Lewin of the N.Y.U. Conservation Center has announced that he has developed a liquid formula that may help to prevent the erosion of stone monuments. The solution is composed of water, barium hydroxide, and urea. When applied to limestone it tends to preserve and extend the life of the object and, in effect, to permit it to heal itself of disease. Six European countries have promised to send specimens of limestone for testing with the new formula.

Experiments are being conducted to find out if a protective cover applied to stone after cleaning will lengthen its life. Research is directed at waxes that are soluble in water and modern synthetic materials but there is no guarantee of success. The real answer, say the experts, is to reduce the amount of pollution in the air by treating industrial smoke before it is discharged or transferring the offending plants and power stations out of urban centers where most monuments are concentrated. Only in this way can such a treasure as the mammoth bronze horses of St. Mark's Cathedral in Venice be saved.

As to the paintings of the masters, the scientists have set up "art hospitals" in Brussels and elsewhere in Europe where canvases are diagnosed and ministered to as carefully as human patients. To preserve or restore their original beauty X-ray photographs taken with infrared, ultraviolet, or fluorescent light are made to reveal the paint layer by layer. Ultramodern tools are used to scrape away paint applied in previous restorations and to get down to the original.

Many times the latest techniques are required to repair the blundering work of amateur restorers in the past. An excellent example of the latter is a copy of Leonardo da Vinci's celebrated mural of "The Last Supper" reproduced by one of his pupils, Andreas Solario. As it traveled from Italy to France to Belgium it was badly damaged, especially when it was buried underground during the French Revolution, and it received even harsher treatment at the hands of past "restorers." For five years or more specialists at the *Institut Royal de Patrimoine Ar-*

tistique in Brussels have been going over the giant canvas inch by inch to correct the errors of former "restorations." It is delicate, meticulous, patient work but when the painting is finished it will again glow with the artistry of the master and his pupil.

Where wood has been used in a statue or other work of art, it has been found that 80 per cent of them are infested with insects which devour their insides. To halt this depredation the experts inject special chemicals which destroy the invaders and prevent reinfestation. If the object has been weakened by the invasion they pump in plastic solutions or emulsions which strengthen it and prolong its life. This treatment has been notably successful in "curing" the ills of the woodwork in Westminster Abbey and the sculptures at the Palace of Versailles among thousands of cases.

The following pages are devoted to a description of fourteen outstanding antiquities throughout the world which have been threatened with death from one cause or another and have been, are being, or will be rescued by modern scientific techniques for the enrichment of future generations.

II

WESTMINSTER ABBEY:
CLEANSED OF
ANCIENT GRIME

⊄ ⊄ ⊄

Westminster Abbey in London is a huge pile of Gothic stone serving partly as royal cathedral, partly as national Pantheon, partly as storehouse of history, and wholly as England's greatest shrine. Virtually every English king and queen has been crowned within its hallowed walls since William the Conqueror in 1066 and most of them are buried there. It is also the tomb of statesmen and soldiers, nobility and commoners, rich and poor, famous and infamous, and a three-day-old infant—the daughter of James I. It is cluttered with monuments to their memory in varying degrees of taste and it reflects the very essence of England for thirty-five generations. Its 900th anniversary fell in 1966 and celebrations were held there throughout the year with Queen Elizabeth heading the procession of notables.

A church has stood on this spot on the left bank of the Thames River since the seventh century but the sainted King Edward the Confessor founded Westminster Abbey in 1065, as we know it today, under the name of the Collegiate Church of St. Peter. Henry III and his son Edward I rebuilt and enlarged it in the thirteenth century and the Chapel of Henry VII was added in the sixteenth century. During the Reformation Henry VIII stripped it of its treasures and reduced it to the status of a minor church in keeping with his abolition of the monasteries. After several centuries of a troubled existence Sir Christopher Wren carried out extensive repairs to its stonework in the eighteenth century and the two western towers were built. At the close of World War I the body of the "Unknown Warrior" was buried there and after World War II a memorial window was installed in honor of the Royal Air Force pilots who died in the Battle of Britain.

Westminster has frequently been a scene of violence and bloodshed as well as pomp and circumstance. As one example, at the coronation of William the Conqueror the audience, including many prominent Britons, was instructed to vote for the king in imitation of a popular election and the question had to be put in both English and French. When the roars of approval went up the Norman soldiers guarding the church misconstrued them as the start of a riot and indulged in a massacre of the people.

A front view of Westminster Abbey in London.

The Abbey is built in the form of a Latin Cross and is 513 feet long, 200 feet wide through the transept, and 102 feet high at the peak of the nave. From its vaulted nave to its smallest chapel it is crammed with richly adorned tombs, statues, sculptures, mosaics, paintings, and assorted bric-a-brac—some of them overly ornate by present standards. Adjoining the structure are a deanery, a museum, and Westminster School which has sent many distinguished graduates into the world.

Standing in the Abbey are row on row of monuments to such soldiers as the Duke of Wellington and Lord Nelson, such statesmen as William Pitt, William Gladstone, and Sir Robert Peel, such scientists as Charles Darwin and Sir Isaac Newton, such writers as Shakespeare, Dickens, Wordsworth, Tennyson, and Thackeray. Entombed there is a long roll call of monarchs like Edward the Confessor himself, buried a week after completion of his dream, Mary Queen of Scots, her mortal enemy Elizabeth I, Henry VII, Richard II, and many others. Almost every modern English notable is buried there or has a statue to his memory.

Edward the Confessor's tomb in Westminster Abbey.

Westminster has a number of American associations. An unhappy one is a monument to Major John André, who was condemned by George Washington as a British spy and executed during the Revolutionary War. A happier one is a memorial plaque honoring Franklin D. Roosevelt as "a faithful friend of freedom and of Britain." Nearby is a marble slab embedded in the floor saying of his wartime friend: "Remember Winston Churchill."

Although Churchill preferred to be buried elsewhere, as Prime Minister he initiated a national campaign in 1953 to raise £1,000,000 (about $2,800,000) to restore and maintain the Abbey and its appendages. In his appeal for funds he said, "Shall we in this valiant generation allow this building to moulder under our eye. Both the monuments and the stonework of centuries are falling into decay and the soot of London must be cleaned away if we are to prevent the stone from crumbling. Our generation would indeed be held to shame by those who came afterwards if we failed to preserve this noble inheritance." Queen Elizabeth was the first to make a contribution and the fund was subscribed to the last shilling. About $1,100,000 was set aside to remove the grime of nine centuries, repair the stonework, repaint the interior, and generally to re-create it in all its past glory. For more than a decade a small army of workmen has been doing the job and the task was completed in time for the 900th anniversary.

When they embarked on the project in 1954 the Abbey was in such a critical state of dilapidation that it was feared it would have to be closed to the public lest someone be killed or injured. During the coronation of the Queen a sixty-foot long parapet had to be shored up as an emergency measure for fear it would fall on the notables. Centuries of smoke, soot, and sulphuric fumes, spewing in the last century from factory smokestacks and automobile exhausts, had eaten away much of the exterior stone. On the interior, pinnacles and balustrades were flaking off, sculptures were crumbling, paintings were losing their color, gilded statues were growing murky, wooden beams were being chewed up by "death-watch beetles."

Marching in the front lines of the attack was a squad of "charwomen" or lady cleaners who attacked the walls with plain soap and water and gave them what was perhaps the biggest bath in history. Swinging their scrub brushes and banging their pails on the floor, they belabored the dark-stained interior and removed literally tons of dirt until it gleamed again with its original whiteness.

Skilled craftsmen, meanwhile, converged on the tombs and monuments and restored many of them to their former brilliance. They repainted, regilded, and repaired the faces and figures of long-dead personages until they glittered again with the colors of old. High on their list were the tombs of those ancient enemies, Elizabeth I and Mary Queen of Scots, whose features seemed to come to life again under their tools.

Other workmen tackled the roofs which were in danger of collapsing. They reconstructed crumbling stone balustrades and recast hundreds of tons of lead sheathing covering the roofs. When they examined the 500-year-

A statue in the Abbey being restored.

Two craftsmen regilding the organ in the Abbey.

old oak timbers supporting the roofs they discovered that most of them had been riddled by "death-watch beetles" and had to be replaced before the other work could go forward. The experts concluded that the roofs would have fallen in in another few years if the condition had not been corrected.

As the work came to an end, sixteen crystal chandeliers of Waterford glass were installed in the soaring nave and it sparkled in splendor. The pillars and walls and spires shone with renewed brightness. The gorgeous rose windows at each end of the transept glowed with beauty. The details of the statues scattered throughout the structure scintillated with polychrome and gold leaf. Westminster Abbey as the Queen's "Royal Peculiar" and the "People's Church" appeared more resplendent than it had for nine hundred years and stood ready for another nine hundred years of glory by the Thames. Its future maintenance has been assured for many years by setting aside an endowment fund.

III

VENICE:

SINKING INTO THE SEA

⊂⊅ ⊂⊅ ⊂⊅

Beautiful Venice, the Queen City of the Adriatic, rose out of the sea like Venus and like Venus may be destined to return to the sea. The first inhabitants were refugees seeking safety from the barbarians of northern Italy in the miserable mud banks of a lagoon just off the mainland at the close of the sixth century. They built their settlement on 117 islands under the name of Rialto, erecting the foundations of their homes on wooden piles.

For six hundred years Venice was a part of the Byzantine Empire at Constantinople but with her trade expanding eastward through the Mediterranean she crushed the pirates of Dalmatia across the water, gradually asserted her independence, and gained control over the Adriatic. By the time of the First Crusade the city-state ruled the sea routes to the Holy Land, held several footholds in the

Levantine states, and reaped great wealth from her trad-
ing activities in the East.

These riches inspired her brilliance as one of the
world's great art capitals. The long list of her talented
architects, painters, and sculptors—Titian above all the
rest—reads like the roll call of the immortals, and their
works span the entire range of the Byzantine, Gothic,
Baroque, early and late Renaissance periods. Under the
patronage of emperors and kings, princes and doges, and
with the leisure generated by the city's commercial
wealth, they created such a treasury of masterpieces that
a walk through Venice is akin to a walk through a com-
bination art gallery and museum.

The incomparable St. Mark's Square, perhaps the best-

St. Mark's Square and its waterfront in Venice.

known and best-loved square in Europe, is a noble introduction to a city that is crisscrossed with more than 150 canals and is punctuated with nearly four hundred bridges. Paved with marble, the Square is 192 yards long and 61 yards and 90 yards wide at either end. Scattered around its borders are the Procuratie or palaces of the nine Procurators who once ruled the Republic. At one end are the rebuilt Campanile or Tower of St. Mark's, and the Clock Tower, which not only tolls the hour but gives the position of the sun and moon. Along one side is the imposing Basilica or Church of St. Mark's flanked by four bronze horses five feet high. Over all flutter the ubiquitous flocks of pigeons which may be picturesque to feed but are also carriers of decay to the city's monuments.

The Church of St. Mark's, named after the patron saint of Venice, was built in the ninth century in the form of a Greek Cross crowned with five domes in the Byzantine style but with later Gothic additions. The structure is embellished inside and out with over five hundred marble columns and with gorgeous mosaics from various periods. It is 83 yards long and 56 yards broad in front and every yard of it is encrusted with gold and bronze decorations. In ancient times it was the official church of the Republic where the reigning Doge attended services in state during important festivals and now it is the cathedral of the Archbishop of Venice.

Just off St. Mark's Square is the lavish Palace of the Doges, built in the nineteenth century for the first Doge and rebuilt several times after fires. This two-story building has a superb Gothic exterior and later touches of the

The Church of St. Mark's.

*The Palace of the Doges, off
St. Mark's Square.*

early Renaissance. Here the Doges were crowned, the decrees of the Republic were proclaimed, and sentences of death were passed.

Elsewhere along the shores of the Grand Canal, the main artery of the city, and other waterways, Venice is filled with palaces, churches, and museums and most of them are crammed with artistic treasures reflecting the glories of her illustrious past. Many of them are remarkably well preserved but some have deteriorated into little more than slums.

Regardless of its past luster the Queen City is facing a dubious future. It is either sinking slowly into its lagoon or the waters of the Adriatic are rising slowly to drown it, or both, according to how you view the evidence. Some surveys show that Venice as a whole has sunk about four

The great staircase of the Palace of the Doges.

inches in the past fifty years but it varies from place to place. The ground beneath the Tower of St. Mark's, which collapsed in 1902 and had to be rebuilt from the ruins, for instance, has sunk about seven inches in that time. Some engineers estimate that the city as a whole has been subsiding at an average rate of about one-tenth of an inch a year.

Every winter the tides of the Adriatic sweep higher and higher into St. Mark's Square, turning the marble expanse in front of the Cathedral into a small lake two and one half feet deep and washing over its entrance steps. In the past seven years there have been twenty-five serious floods.

Mellow old monuments such as the Fortress of Ste. Andrea at the entrance to the port have had their walls split open by the creeping waters and have begun to fall into the sea. (This is the fort from which Casanova, the notorious adventurer, is supposed to have escaped after conviction for an infraction of the law.)

The assault on Venice comes not only from the sea. Whereas the original canals were carved out in conformity with the currents of the lagoon, new ones have been artificially plotted in a straight line and are exposed to a greater impact of the ebb and flow of the tides, eating away at the foundation and sub-foundation of the city. The fleets of large motorboats (Vaporettas) and small speedboats (Motoscafi) which are rapidly replacing the traditional gondolas of romantic memory are also contributing to the decline. The wash of their powerful engines surges from one side of the canals to the other,

The Tower of St. Mark's in St. Mark's Square.

The broken walls of the Fortress of Ste. Andrea at the entrance to the port.

gnawing away at the city's underpinnings. Every city has its traffic problems but in a city which bans the motor car out of necessity this problem is unique.

Venice is also under attack from other enemies: salt water erosion, the ejection of motorboat fuel oil, industrial pollution from the air, and even the droppings of the beloved pigeons. All these combine to erode the city's foundation and crumble the facades of its monuments. As the movement of the tides carries sand from one part of the lagoon bed to another, the Lido Beach, once the most famous in Europe, has been shrunk to a narrow ribbon of sand. Of Venice's two hundred palaces it is calculated that about 50 per cent stand in need of repair and of her 110 churches at least 10 per cent are almost beyond reconstruction.

In the face of these dangers a national city planning organization called *Italia Nostra* (Our Italy) was set up in 1958 and its first goal was to preserve and restore the historic heart of Venice with most of its monuments and to combat plans to commercialize it. The Municipal Council, supported by the city's business interests, had just approved a master plan of civic improvement to allow automobiles into the city for the first time by building a highway from the mainland, to erect skyscrapers which would overshadow the great palaces, and to create an administrative center on the islands. The two forces clashed head-on in a battle royal.

Both sides recognized that Venice, aside from its other afflictions, was in deep economic trouble and neither wished to turn it into a "Museum City" with all its citizens cast in the role of guides or gondoliers. Old Venice was losing residents at the rate of 2,500 to 3,000 a year and the population had been reduced to about 125,000 from a 1952 peak of around 175,000 while the industrial suburb of Mestre and the port of Marghera on the mainland were gaining in proportion. The "modernists" argued that the city was stagnating outside the tourist season and that it needed a transfusion of industrial blood. The "traditionalists" replied that the proposed changes would destroy the cultural atmosphere of the city and would drive away the lucrative tourist trade without bringing compensating revenue.

To hold back the sea Italia Nostra countered with a proposal that locks be placed at the main entrance to the

On the Grand Canal in Venice.

A palace on the Grand Canal in the process of deterioration.

lagoon to control the water level and prevent high tides.
To improve the economic health of the city, it proposed
that Venice be transformed into an international center
on the order of Geneva to accommodate cultural conven-
tions. To halt the outward flow of Venetians it proposed
that a new residential suburb be built between the city
and nearby Mestre. To stop the deterioration of the city,
it proposed a program of strict zoning and slum clearance
which would raze nondescript structures of recent origin

but would save genuine old villas. To block the advance of industry, it proposed that large factories be restricted to the mainland but that small, non-polluting plants be permitted in certain sections. In general, it was proposing a Greater Venice with a careful balance between culture and commerce—each in its proper place.

Famous architects like Frank Lloyd Wright and Le Corbusier and writers such as Ernest Hemingway sided with Italia Nostra for the most part but real estate, shipping and manufacturing interests fought the suggestions fang and claw. Their struggle stirred up a torrent of public debate in the press and generated many private maneuvers behind the scenes, cutting across political lines and even dividing prominent families over a period of several years. At length, the Municipal Council caved in and reversed itself, partially under pressure from the Ministry of Public Works in Rome. Most of Italia Nostra's ideas were accepted but they have yet to be put into practice. The latter recognizes that a conflict such as this is never finally settled and maintains constant vigilance to protect its victory.

As a supporter of Italia Nostra, Pietro Gazzola, State Inspector of Fine Arts and Antiques and one of the most respected authorities in Italy on the subject, lists five causes for the perilous condition of Venice: 1. The slow submergence of the bed of the lagoon due to unnatural hydraulic practices. 2. The erosion of the canals' underpinnings as a result of the motorboats' operations and other causes. 3. Lack of maintenance of the larger monuments. 4. The concentration of the populace in a restricted area, shutting out light and air. 5. The deterioration of the smaller structures to the extent that whole areas have been turned into near-slums.

"Venice, to survive, must have a complete and sane plan," he contends, "in which each of the separate problems is confronted and all the aspects of the situation are covered. The reclaiming of the lagoon calls for different measures according to the particular zone. The reform of the various means of transportation must be carefully studied and weighed against the characteristics of the canals and the houses and, above all, the vulnerability of the under-foundations.

"Every people, every man has a long-standing and contingent debt to Venice. Civilization itself has a debt not easily put aside. It appears clear that only a supranational organization such as UNESCO is capable of representing all those who today, as well as yesterday and tomorrow, look to Venice as the most dramatic expression of the intelligence and spirit of mankind."

A row of disintegrating villas in Venice.

Under the stimulus of Prof. Gazzola, Italia Nostra and other civic-minded elements, the Italian government has set aside more than $1,000,000 for the use of a commission to study methods of curing Venice of her ailments. While the commission argues and deliberates these days, the waters rise ever so slowly in the lagoon, the motorboats roar up and down the canals, the monuments crumble imperceptibly under erosion and the pigeons wheel in the sky over St. Mark's but no concrete steps have been taken to preserve the Queen City for posterity.

The Palace of Gold on St. Mark's Square.

IV

PISA'S LEANING TOWER: TILTING TOWARD DISASTER

₵ ₵ ₵

A few miles inland from the sparkling blue waters of the Ligurian Sea in northern Italy stands a gleaming white cylindrical monument which is one of the landmarks of Europe. This is the famed eight-story medieval Campanile or Leaning Tower of Pisa. Made entirely of marble, it is 179 feet high, 62 feet in diameter at its widest point and more than 17 feet out of plumb. Whether or not it will eventually fall over and crash in ruins has been a subject of heated controversy since the day it was built in the twelfth century.

The Leaning Tower dates from Pisa's Golden Age when, as one of the Italian city-states, her galleys ruled the Mediterranean from Spain to Palestine for several centuries. Sometimes allied with Genoa and later ranged against her, Pisa repelled the Saracen thrust from Africa and defeated their forces in Sicily and Sardinia in the eleventh century. At the start of the twelfth century she joined in the Second Crusade to drive the Moslems out of the Holy Land, was represented at the capture of Jerusalem and emerged with great religious and commercial prestige.

For the next four hundred years Pisa fought a series of intermittent wars with the states of Genoa, Florence, and Lucca, sometimes winning and sometimes losing but always growing weaker, and finally the Florentines destroyed her power for all time in 1509.

At the zenith of her glory, however, Pisa was rich beyond the dreams of Croesus and she displayed her wealth by adorning the city with a complex of noble buildings along the river Arno. The most imposing of these were the Cathedral, the Baptistery, and the Campanile itself clustered together in the northwest section of the city. As designed by Pisan architects, the Cathedral was built in the form of a Latin cross 312 feet long and 252 feet wide across the interior transepts. The Baptistery was created as a circle 100 feet in diameter and surmounted with a dome 190 feet high, topped by the statue of a saint. Both were made of black and white marble and neither has ever shown any sign of a slant.

An architect named Bonanno Pisano started the construction of the Campanile in 1174 to match the other structures. He sank his foundation nine feet into the soft, volcanic soil, which was as deep as he could go because of

The Cathedral and Leaning Tower of Pisa.

The Church of St. Paul on the River Arno in Pisa.

the level of the sea, and he had raised the base not more than forty feet when he found it had already developed a list. He tried to compensate for this by building the first three stories at a slight angle, much as a child might try to correct the tilt in a pile of blocks, but it did no good and he abandoned the job.

A century later another architect, Giovanni di Simone, took over the project and, assuming that the soil had settled, completed four more stories but he discovered that the lean—far from being arrested—had increased perceptibly. Seventy-five years later a third architect, Tomasso Pisano, added the eighth story or cupola to house the bells, completing the tower in 1350 as we see it today, but the tilt continued because of the porous state of the soil.

The tower's list and the resultant fear of visitors have tended to catalogue it as a freak and obscure its real beauty. Its base is encircled by semi-circular arches supported by fifteen columns, its six arcades above this are supported by thirty columns each, and the top story is much smaller than the rest with twelve columns. The thickness of its wall varies from 13 feet at the bottom to 8 feet at the top and its total weight is 15,000 tons. Boring through the structure is a spiral stairway with 275 short steps, somewhat similar to those of the Statue of Liberty (which is 151 feet high and has 335 steps), but much easier to climb, which lead upward as far as the bell compartment. The latter holds seven bells, one of which weighs five tons, and they were tolled in celebration of maritime victories in olden days but this has long since been stopped for fear of vibration.

The Leaning Tower was 15½ feet out of perpendicular by 1829 and since then the rate of incline has been mounting. Since 1918, the first year in which scientific measurements were used by the University of Pisa, the inclination has grown at the rate of about .04 inches a year. Some authorities draw the conclusion from these figures that the tower is in little or no danger of falling and might stand forever even if nothing is done. Others contend that it might topple over tomorrow in a strong wind and there is no time to lose in taking corrective measures. Regardless of their opinions, all recall that the Tower of St. Mark's in Venice suddenly collapsed in 1902 and had to be rebuilt from the rubble.

Thousands of proposals for saving the tower have come in from all over the world in the past eight hundred years. Some of them have been based on sound engineering principle and others have been products of fertile imaginations. A few of them have been put into practice but they did not correct the list and in several cases they increased it. The last attempt was in 1935 when Benito Mussolini sent a team of experts to inject cement into the soil beneath the tower to waterproof its foundation.

Among the ideas advanced from time to time for rescuing the tower have been: Freeze it in a block of ice and lift it off the ground while its foundation is being reinforced; hitch on a couple of locomotives and pull it back into plumb; attach barrage balloons to the top and hold it in place; dig out a hunk of soil on the side opposite the lean and let it settle back into place. None of these has been entertained seriously.

The Leaning Tower, with the Baptistery in the background.

One proposal put forward recently by Gustavo Colo-
netti, former president of the Italian National Research
Council, is under serious consideration. He suggests cir-
cling the tower with fifteen enormous hydraulic jacks,
each capable of lifting one thousand tons, or the total
weight of the mass. Cables from the jacks would be
hitched to a steel jacket enveloping the base of the tower.
Then the jacks operating in synchronism would lift the
tower ever so slowly straight into the air until a few
inches clearance had been gained. At that point workmen
could step in and lay a new foundation. "This would be
such a delicate, such a beautiful operation," says Dr. Colo-
netti.

Although the experts may disagree on the remedy they
are in unanimous agreement on the patient's illness. The
subsoil beneath the tower is a porous mixture of sand and
clay, irrigated by spring water seeping from the nearby
river, and should never have been expected to bear its
weight. The Cathedral, the Baptistery, and several of the
buildings in Pisa also list slightly but their weight, in com-
parison with their height, is better distributed over their
foundations.

Several years ago the Ministry of Public Works, the
office charged with responsibility for the large-scale preservation of monuments, appointed the latest of a series of
commissions to study the problem and recommend a solution. At the same time they announced an international
contest to generate new salvage proposals from the public and a new crop of ideas has been flooding in. There was
also talk of submitting a bill to Parliament to appropriate

$3,000,000 for the reconstruction work but nothing has come of this.

Whatever happens as a result of all these schemes, literally no one favors a plan to *straighten* the tower—only to arrest the tilt where it is. Several million tourists come to visit the phenomenon every year, most of them to photograph it and pass on but others to remain overnight, and their expenditures shower a tidy income on the city. If the Tower were ever made too safe, the Pisans reason, it would destroy the suspenseful sense of danger and might dam up the golden flow of cash.

Prof. Piero Sanpaolesi, director of the Institute for Restoration of Monuments in Florence and formerly superintendent of monuments in Pisa, has written a book on the Tower which closes with some poignant remarks about its long-muted bells: "These bells have been silent for more than a hundred years because of the danger that their ringing might topple the tower. The promise that on some not-too-distant Holy Saturday we may enjoy again the full concert of these famous bells should urge us prudently but energetically to seek the solution that will dispel for all time the danger to our beautiful Tower."

V

MONT-SAINT-MICHEL: RECAPTURED FROM DESPOILERS

⊂⊅ ⊂⊅ ⊂⊅

Mont-Saint-Michel, one of the wonders of France, stands like a lonely sentinel guarding the rocky coast of Normandy. It is a forbidding mask of cone-shaped granite about 3,000 feet in circumference and about 165 feet high lying on an inlet a mile off shore in the Gulf of St. Malo. At its summit are the Abbey of Mont-Saint-Michel and other religious buildings and at its base huddles a small village with a few hundred souls.

Mont-Saint-Michel entered history in 708 when St. Aubert, Bishop of Avranches, built an oratory or chapel on command of the Archangel Michael who was reputed to have appeared to him in a vision. Two centuries later Richard I, Duke of Normandy, founded a Benedictine abbey in 966 and a hundred years later the monks aided William the Conqueror in the conquest of England by sending six armed ships. When the English in turn occupied Normandy, the French King Phillip II burned the monastery in 1203 but after he dislodged the enemy he had it restored. Under Napoleon Bonaparte the abbey was turned into a prison, was allowed to disintegrate and endured a shameful period until 1863 when it was taken over by the state and returned to religious purposes. During World War II it was used as an observation post by the Germans but emerged undamaged from the Allied liberation of France.

Mont-Saint-Michel guarding the coast of Normandy.

Today the noble edifices of Mont-Saint-Michel, many of them hewn out of the rock, represent a cross-section of French architecture from the tenth century Carolingian, through the Roman, Gothic in all its stages, up to the eighteenth century Classic, but most of the buildings have their roots in the eleventh to thirteenth centuries.

Outstanding among them is "La Merveille" or "Marvel," a jumble of six buildings which rise on three levels facing the sea.

Crowning the "Marvel" is the church proper which was started in the Norman style in the tenth century, underwent many modifications and was finished in the Gothic style in the fifteenth century. Its choir and chapels are especially notable for their scriptures and bas-reliefs. The central tower has been rebuilt in the original style with a Gothic spire and the latter is surmounted by a gilded bronze statue of St. Michael flying aloft at a height of 510 feet.

Since its birth the abbey has been a shrine for pilgrims from many parts of Europe, and in the early days many were drowned crossing a mile of angry water to the isle, earning it the name of "Saint Michel of-the-Peril-of-the-Sea." But a causeway was built in 1879 across the Bay of Saint Michel to connect it permanently with the village of Pontorson and the mainland and the only danger now is wet feet from the tides.

Mont-Saint-Michel has been going through a process of restoration for a hundred years since the departure of its last convict and it has finally been rescued from its uncouth despoilers and well-intentioned friends alike

view of Mont-Saint-Michel showing the causeway connecting it to the ainland.

through the efforts of the *Service des Monuments Historiques*. The first architect on the job constructed a solid buttress at one corner of the abbey to prevent it from collapsing, consolidated the foundations and walls, and waterproofed one terrace, saving the whole from imminent destruction. Turning to the "Marvel," he tore out a crude flooring marring the refectory and a nest of prisoners' cells profaning the cloister and reestablished the original architectural design.

Later architects reinforced the pillars of the transept in the abbey and reconstructed the bell tower and wooden spire. By that time reinforced concrete had appeared on

The refectory of Mont-Saint-Michel after restoration.

the scene and this was freely employed to restore the chapels, dormitories, and promenades, returning the church to something approaching its original aspect.

In recent years the architects turned their attention to the other buildings surrounding the abbey, some of which had been desecrated by their use as detention cells, and, after reference to the original plans, they painstakingly restored their chambers to the religious purposes for which they were built. In the course of this work they came upon the vestiges of an old pre-Roman church beneath the abbey, disentangled it from other structures, and put it back in service.

The final works of restoration were to return the roof of the cloister to its original state by replacing its glazed tiles with a thick rock-covering affixed with mortar to resist the tug of the sea winds, and to replant the garden in the center which was first laid out in the seventeenth century.

Serious attempts were made to clean up the surroundings of the abbey and the "Marvel" which had been pock-marked by unsightly commercial structures and cheap souvenir shops. Some of them were acquired by the state and demolished and a zoning code was introduced to control the more blatant operators but the village still has its share of honky-tonk emporia.

Reviewing the work of restoration, Yves-Marie Froidevaux, chief architect of the Monuments' Service, comments: "From the beginning the guiding principal was to maintain a prudent reserve and the innovations were limited to those that were indispensable for assuring the stability and the proper emphasis on points of architectural or historical interest which had been compromised by latter-day worthless transformation. . . . For in addition to the abstract goal of converting the architectural structure, restoration of a monument must have a direction. Even inhabited Mont-Saint-Michel must live in the hearts of all as a living image of a great monastery built to welcome pilgrims of the Archangel."

VI

LASCAUX CAVE PAINTINGS: SAVED FROM THE GREEN MOLD

One day in September, 1940, four boys saw a dog disappear into the side of a hill near Périgueux in the Dordogne region of southwest France. When they followed it into the opening they found that it led into an enormous cavern whose walls were lined with some extraordinary paintings. After experts had examined them they told the lads they had stumbled on the most important works of prehistoric man in existence between fifteen thousand and twenty thousand years old. For these were the now famous cave murals of Lascaux.

When the experts had recovered from their astonishment and ceased congratulating each other on this stroke of luck they began to take inventory of the remarkable discovery. As to the layout of the cavern, they determined that the first section was the Main Hall or "Hall of the Bulls," measuring some thirty feet across and about one hundred feet deep. This led directly into a long narrow, dead-end corridor which they labeled the "Axial Gallery." Branching off on one side of the Main Hall was another narrow passage running into what was named the "Nave" and the "Apse" in terms of church architecture. Almost every foot of these walls was covered with such a profusion of paintings of animal life, as vivid and as fresh as the day they were done, that the ensemble was christened the "Sistine Chapel of Pre-History" in token of its importance to the art world.

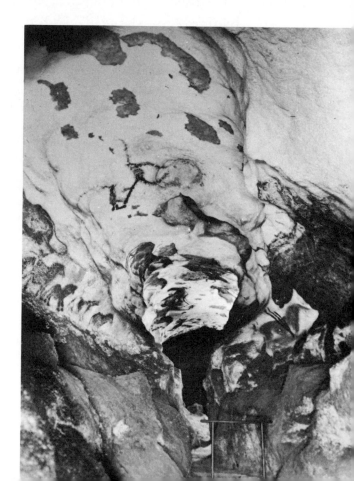

A wall of the Lascaux caves showing paintings of bulls, cows, and horses.

As one entered the Hall of the Bulls one's eyes were transfixed by a long panel of animals dominated by four gigantic bulls painted in brilliant reds, yellows, and browns. Headed by an eight-foot long "unicorn," a procession of bulls, horses, deer, and cows follows one another along the entire length of one wall and circles back along another. Unlike most primitive representation, they are not flat and stiff but so artfully created that they offer an almost three-dimensional effect.

The walls of the Axial Gallery were embellished with a second menagerie of animals, among them small "Chinese" horses, cows, and ibexes, galloping, leaping, and falling head over heels in wild abandon. Here are the dramatic "Frieze of the Little Horses," a superb black bull and other strange, fanciful beasts. The Nave is populated by figures of a large black cow, a pair of bison, and a frieze of five deer heads. Leading off the Nave down a low tunnel to a slippery incline, is a small cave called the "Room of the Felines" in recognition of faint etchings of cat-like creatures.

The talent displayed in these murals raises the question as to what manner of human was a Lascaux man? He apparently lived during the upper Paleolithic or late Stone Age. His body was similar to that of modern man, his forehead was high, and he had a trim, narrow jaw. His native intelligence was roughly equal to ours and he was gifted with creative genius. The anthropological evidence appears to be positive that he was the first species of man capable of turning out a work of art.

Georges Bataille, writing in his authoritative *Lascaux or*

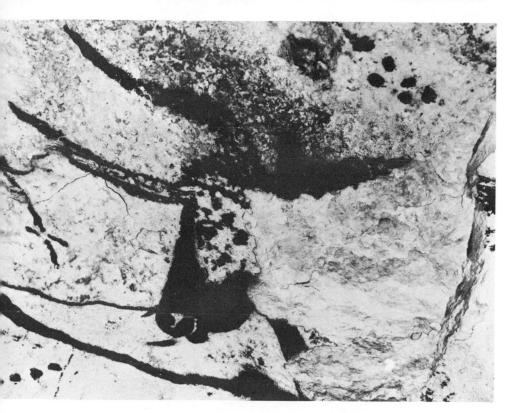

The painting of the black bull in the Axial Gallery.

Paintings of bulls and horses in the Hall of the Bulls.

the Birth of Art, describes Lascaux man and his works thus: "Taken as a whole, Lascaux' paintings, while perhaps not the oldest, form the finest and most intact group we have. Indeed, we may say that nothing tells us more about the life and thought of those men who were the first to have the power to deliver themselves of that profound but enigmatic utterance, a detached work of art. These paintings before us are miraculous, they communicate a strong and intimate emotion."

The public agreed with the experts and journeyed to the Lascaux caves by the thousands to feast their eyes and enrich their souls in front of the artistic marvels. In one recent year more than 120,000 persons, among them many Americans, paid a pilgrimage to the shrine, as many as five hundred visitors a day trooped through the corridors, and it became the fourth most popular tourist lure in France. A new lighting system was installed a few years ago where only darkness had reigned for centuries and air-conditioning was introduced for the comfort of guests and guides alike.

Some years ago, however, French archaeologists began to complain that the colors of the paintings, especially the reds, were fading and the first faint sounds of alarm began to reverberate. By the spring of 1963 fears for the safety of the works became a national concern and the authorities closed the caves temporarily while they investigated the causes of the trouble. They discovered that a green mold composed of algae, a microscopic sea plant, was slowly spreading over the walls and destroying the paintings.

The French Minister of Cultural Affairs, André Malraux, named a mission of leading scientists to conduct a study of the situation from every point of view. Its preliminary findings were that the atmospheric balance of the cavern had been disturbed by the presence of visitors after thousands of years of isolation. They speculated that the latter might have brought in germs on their clothing or that their very breathing might have infected the atmosphere. Other speculations were that the lighting and air-conditioning systems might be responsible for the malady.

As the green mold, or *le mal vert* as the French say, spread with lightning-like speed, the caves were barred to the public for an indefinite period and there is doubt that they will ever be reopened. With the grotto hermetically

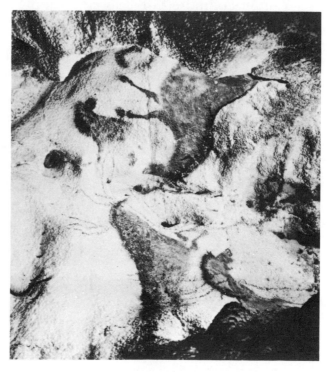

A painting of a "falling" horse at Lascaux

sealed, the scientists set about to restore its "living conditions" as they had existed for millennia. They experimented with measures to disinfect the air, re-create the physical-climatic balance, and applied chemicals to the paintings to arrest the growth of the fungi.

Then the Commission went into action against the "enemy" on all fronts. They first drafted a battle map on which the strong points of the disease were marked, listing a set of priorities according to its progression, and posted nine hundred coded reference marks on the walls of the cave. The scientists injected into the ventilating system a mixture called the "Pochon Cocktail"—named after a member of the team—consisting of 600 million units of penicillin, thirty grams of streptomycin and thirty grams of kanamycine to sterilize the atmosphere. Next they brushed on or sprayed on the paintings a potion composed of diluted formol, in its natural state or combined with other chemicals, to all the diseased spots, sometimes applying two or three applications to root out the infection. The graphs on the "patient's" chart began to fall from fourteen hundred areas of contamination to seven hundred to near zero with only a few algae holding out against the treatment. The statistics of victory over the "villain" rose from 60 per cent to 85 per cent to nearly 100 per cent. The day finally came after two years of struggle when the soldiers of science announced wearily that the conflict was won—the paintings had been saved for posterity.

As the weeks passed the "patient" entered into a period of convalescence while the scientists pondered its future. In the course of their research they had discovered that the walls of the cave were subject to calcification and the paintings were subject to fading. They had cured one illness only to be plagued by another. But this was essentially a disease of old age and could be arrested only by restricting the number of visitors to the minimum.

While the public at large may never again be admitted to the cavern, several ingenious schemes have been advanced to give visitors a simulated tour. One proposal is to dig another cave in the same hill as an exact copy of the original and exhibit color photographs of the paintings. Another is to make an extensive film of the art and show it in an unaffected section of the grotto. Still another is to combine these ideas by creating a new cave and projecting televised views of the murals. Whichever scheme is adopted, scientists and scholars may be permitted access to the original in limited numbers from time to time but the day of unlimited hordes of tourists is over. Their disappointment may be tempered by the knowledge that the incomparable cave paintings of Lascaux will be preserved for generations to come.

VII

THE PARTHENON: CRUMBLING BIT BY BIT

⊂⊧ ⊂⊧ ⊂⊧

The 2400-year-old Parthenon sits atop the Acropolis in the heart of Athens like a diadem gracing the head of a beautiful queen. The temple was built during the Golden Age of Pericles when the Greek city-state attained the highest point of her mastery in the arts, sciences, humanities, and political democracy. Pericles himself had a hand in its creation and his good friend Phidias, the illustrious sculptor, designed the statuary. It was dedicated as a shrine to the Goddess Athena and she was worshiped there for six centuries. After Greece accepted Christianity it was converted into a church in about the fifth century and was consecrated to the Virgin Mary. In the fifteenth century when the Ottoman Turks subjugated the Greeks the church was turned into a mosque and a minaret was erected over it.

When the Venetians attacked Athens in the seventeenth century the Turks entrenched themselves on the Acropolis and used the Parthenon as a powder magazine. The attackers blew up the interior of the temple with their artillery, killing three hundred men, and the Turkish commander surrendered. The Venetians sought to transport some of the sculptures to Venice but they were shattered during removal due to the clumsiness of the workmen. During the Greek War of Independence early in the nineteenth century the temple was again damaged but not as seriously. Since then there have been several plans to reconstruct it and it has been patched up from time to time but it has never been restored to its original grandeur.

The Acropolis in Athens, crowned by the Parthenon.

The British Ambassador, Lord Elgin, persuaded the Turkish Sultan to sell many of its art treasures to his government and they now rest in the British Museum in London under the name of the "Elgin Marbles," among its proudest possessions.

The Parthenon has been described as the most perfect object ever wrought by the hand of man and even in ruins it displays the hallmark of genius. As originally built of Pentelic marble dug out of nearby Mt. Pentelicon, it was made up of sixty-two large and thirty-six small columns, about fifty life-sized statues on the pediments, a frieze 524 feet in length, ninety-two metopes or smaller statues, and a figure of Athena 39 feet high. The platform on which it was raised was 228 feet long and 101 feet wide. This was the base for forty-six graceful Doric columns forming the outer framework. The columns tapered gradually toward the top and showed a slight con-

The Parthenon under restoration.

A view of the Parthenon showing fragments of deteriorated stone.

vexity or swelling (entasis) in the middle which gave them an appearance of grace and strength. The inner sanctuary contained the lovely gold and ivory statue of Athena, the greatest work of Phidias. The huge statues adorning the pediments were covered with a fortune in ivory and gold. The reliefs on the smaller statues depicted the struggles of the gods with the giants. The frieze encircling the top of the structure pictured a festive procession approaching the temple to bring gifts to Athena.

The Parthenon looked out as it does today on a collection of magnificent monuments scattered about the Acropolis, which were built about the same time—also of marble.

Now the ruins of the Parthenon and its sister temples are in danger of complete disintegration from a variety of causes. Rain, wind, sun, vegetation, rust, modern invention, and the mere passage of twenty-four centuries have all conspired to erode the monuments and lead the archaeologists to sound the alarm before the process of decay has gone too far.

The Greek government has named a commission to look into the matter and make recommendations for the preservation of the treasures. They are in agreement that the Parthenon is not going to collapse tomorrow, or even in twenty years, but they insist that corrective steps must be taken soon to stop the slow rot.

The most obvious villain in the case is the gentle rain of Attica which seeps into the marble and cracks it, especially after the not-so-gentle sun comes out and raises the temperature. Over a period of years a small crack becomes a fissure and then a deep crevice. First a flake of stone falls off, then a splinter and finally a chunk until the whole mass is crumbling bit by bit. After a cold rain it is a common sight in Athens to see small piles of fallen stone scattered around the base of the columns and workmen filling in the holes with cement or sticking back the larger fragments. These are only stopgap measures which do not go to the heart of the trouble.

Experiments have been made with paraffin and other substances to protect the marble from corrosion but they were not effective and the only result was that the stone turned black and lost its mellow patina. There was an appeal to large chemical firms in the United States and elsewhere to put their research laboratories to work developing an agent that will preserve marble and at the same time not destroy its patina. (Experiments are going on in this field at the N.Y.U. Institute of Fine Arts and at other institutions in Europe.)

An equally serious problem, the archaeologists contend, is that the rain has eroded the exposed limestone foundations of the Parthenon and the other monuments over a long stretch of time. The porous stone is decaying so seriously that it is feared the foundations may not be able to bear the weight of their structures sometime in

A close-up of the columns of the Parthenon.

the future. This condition may call for massive injections of cement to strengthen the foundations or for re-burying them as they were in olden times before they were excavated.

Another cause of concern is the rusting of the iron dowels and clamps inserted in the temples by a team of restorers early in the century and which are now threatening to break the marble apart. To correct this it would be necessary to dismantle all the monuments, replace the iron parts with bronze, as a rust-proof metal, and reassemble them—an enormous task which would take years to complete. The ancient Greek builders covered their joints with lead to prevent oxydization and this recalls a celebrated legend of the Greek War of Independence. When the Turks began stripping the statuary of the lead to make bullets while under siege on the Acropolis the attacking Greeks sent them a memorable message: "Don't destroy the Acropolis. We are sending you bullets," or so the story goes.

Even the wind blows ill for the Parthenon and its companions. It deposits a moldy lichen or fungus on the monuments which forms incrustations on the marble and creeps into the cracks, causing it to splinter and peel. The experts tried using a flame-throwing gun on these growths but this was stopped when it was found that it might damage the marble more than the vegetation—and the Acropolis has seen more than enough fire in its long history.

Some authorities believe that one of the greatest dangers to the Parthenon comes from the skies in the form of the jet plane, and low-altitude flights over the Acropolis have been banned. It is feared that supersonic aircraft, when they enter service in a few years, may further disturb the balance of the various parts of the temples and contribute to their collapse.

If the Commission comes out with a strong bill of remedies to prolong the life of the Parthenon and the rest of the Acropolis, it may be fervently hoped that the temples will survive for another twenty-four hundred years and continue to spread their mantle of beauty in the heart of Athens.

Nike Temple on the Acropolis.

VIII

APHRODISIAS: RESCUED

FROM SQUATTERS

⊂⊉ ⊂⊉ ⊂⊉

As the capital of the ancient Kingdom of Caria the splendorous, all-marble city of Aphrodisias flourished among the olive groves of southwest Asia Minor (near the winding Meander River whence comes our English word "to wander") several hundred years before Christ. It was dedicated to Aphrodite, the Greek goddess of love and beauty, and it was a great cultural center. During the Greek and Roman periods it was a fountainhead of art and sculpture, music and drama, philosophy, oratory, and medicine, and when Byzantium ruled the Orient it became an influential seat of Christianity. Aphrodisias owed much of its prosperity to rich veins of marble located nearby. Every single structure was built of marble and its sculptors sent their works all over the Mediterranean world.

The Roman dictator Sulla thought so highly of Aphrodisias and its works that he sent a golden crown and a double axe as an offering to honor Aphrodite in the first century B.C. A few years later Julius Caesar and other emperors granted freedom and autonomy to the city, exempting it from paying tribute to Rome, and extended to its sanctuary the right of asylum.

Sometime after the eleventh century A.D. Aphrodisias fell into the clutches of the Seljuk Turks, the city rapidly decayed and the site was abandoned. Within the noble marble ruins a few Turkish peasants settled down and a small, nondescript village called Geyre sprang up several hundred years ago. As with peasants everywhere in the Near East, the squatters appropriated priceless works of art and adapted them to their daily life. They used magnificent marble columns to prop up their wooden buildings, employed beautifully carved sculptures for practical purposes, and decorated their homes and barns with delicate reliefs. Aphrodisias' ancient glory had become only a wistful memory but its relics survived amid the cows and chickens of Geyre.

Such was the melancholy state of affairs in 1951 when a team of archaeologists from New York University led by Dr. Kenan T. Erim, associate professor of classics, moved onto the scene to excavate and restore the ruins of Aphrodisias. For the next five years they uncovered a glittering world of wonders from the Hellenic period with the support of the Turkish government. The site covered 220 acres lying in the shadow of snow-clad Baba Dag, a peak in the Aydin mountains of Aegean Turkey, about 140 miles south of Izmir.

One of the first and most interesting discoveries they

made was that of an enormous sports stadium which could seat thirty thousand spectators in its heyday and was still reasonably well preserved. They found it to be one of the most imposing in all the Mediterranean area and comparable to the more famous Greek stadium at Olympia, the seat of the Olympian games. Equally exciting was the discovery of an open-air theater with seats for ten thousand which reminded them of the celebrated Greek theater at Epidaurus. Another find was a small, semicircular, covered odeon or auditorium, in an excellent state of preservation which apparently had been used for lectures, concerts, and other cultural gatherings.

The New York University excavators dug up so many huge marble statues at Aphrodisias that it became

The open-air theater at Aphrodisias.

known as a "mine of statuary." The most spectacular example perhaps was a figure of the cult image of Aphrodite
in three large fragments with the face, headdress, and
arms missing. When the statue stood erect in its original
splendor it must have been nearly ten feet in height and it
is believed to be the only large-sized image of Aphrodite
ever found.

*The upper torso of the famous
statue of Aphrodite found at
Aphrodisias.*

*The lower body of the Aphro-
dite figure.*

The discovery of the so-called "Bishop's Palace," a semi-religious building, was one of the highlights of the operation. Deposits of artifacts from the late Roman and early Byzantine periods indicated that it probably was the residence of a Metropolitan Bishop of Caria or some other high church official sometime between the eleventh

The "Bishop's Palace" at Aphrodisias, with the Temple of Aphrodite in the background.

The Temple of Aphrodite in the background and the "Bishop's Palace" in the foreground.

and fourteenth centuries. They also excavated the remnants of the "Baths of Hadrian," a complex of impressive buildings with a well-preserved central gallery, chambers, and tunnels, and it was considered an ideal site for the erection of a small museum for exhibiting finds of sculpture.

Their most dramatic discovery, however, was the ruins of the temple of Aphrodite, built in the second century A.D., with fourteen of its original Ionic columns still standing proudly in the center of a grove of poplars. They found clear evidence that the structure had been converted into a church in the fourth or fifth century with the coming of Christianity to Asia Minor.

"Few contemporary works found elsewhere," says Dr. Erim, "can vie with the consistent beauty and remarkable execution of the Aphrodisian statuary."

Early in their labors at Aphrodisias Dr. Erim and his colleagues found they could not excavate or preserve the monuments unless the residents of Geyre were removed and the Turkish government came to their aid. The authorities built a model village about a mile away with modern dwellings, barns, storehouses, a mosque, school, and clinic, all surrounded by pastureland on which their livestock could roam and feed. A majority of the villagers gladly moved to the new site but a substantial number still clung to their old homes amid the stately ruins.

Even after the exodus about three-quarters of the site consisting of farmlands, grazing fields, and poplar groves remained in private hands and this posed a serious ob-

The Temple of Aphrodite.

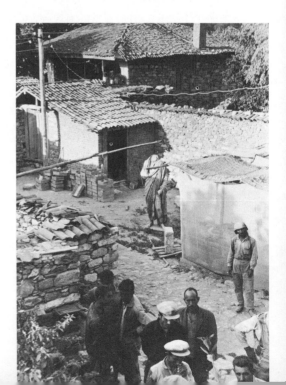

Workmen at Aphrodisias waiting for their superintendent.

stacle to the progress of the restoration work. The expedition insisted the Turkish government must purchase all this land under the right of expropriation and dispossess its tenants regardless of howls of protest. Once this was done, the whole area could be sealed off and converted into an archaeological park. If their plea is successful, Aphrodisias may stand out for centuries to come as an example of a great complex of monuments saved from the squatters' clutches and the squatters themselves may find they are happier in a modern setting.

IX

THE HOLY SEPULCHRE: AN ANCIENT CHURCH REBORN

❧ ❧ ❧

The eight-hundred-year-old Church of the Holy Sepulchre with its twin domes and twin crosses stands in the middle of the Old Walled City of Jerusalem (Jordan) as it has since the Crusades. Covering the supposed site of the Crucifixion, Burial, and Resurrection of Christ, it is perhaps the most sacred shrine in Christendom and has been a magnet for pilgrims for centuries.

The church is an undistinguished, muddy-gray structure situated at the corner of Christian Street and the Via Dolorosa, along which Jesus stumbled on the way to Calvary. Its interior is divided between a circular, domed enclosure and a rectangular building constituting the church proper. Within it are the last five Stations of the

Cross, including the Rock of Golgotha on which He died, and a tiny crypt where He was laid to rest, the Greek Katholikon or Cathedral which forms the nave, the Rotunda, numerous chapels in which the various sects worship, and living quarters for the monks. It is a dark and gloomy place always lighted by flickering candles and it has often been sullied by religious quarrels.

The history of the Holy Sepulchre actually dates back before the Crusades to the fourth century A.D. During that period the Empress Helena of Byzantium made a pilgrimage to Jerusalem and discovered what she held to be the true Cross of Christ. On her return to Constantinople she prevailed on her son, Emperor Constantine, the first Christian ruler of the Roman Empire, to build a church on the site of the Crucifixion. Some three hundred years later

The Church of the Holy Sepulchre in Jerusalem.

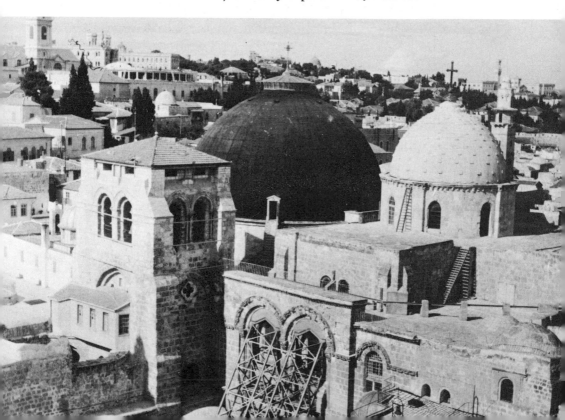

the Persians sacked Jerusalem and destroyed the church, along with every other Christian shrine, but within a few years it was rebuilt even greater than before. When the Moslem Caliph Omar captured the city in the seventh century as part of the Arab conquest of the Holy Land he refused to enter the church and offered his prayers outside as a signal to his followers that it should be preserved as a Christian sanctuary. For the next five hundred years the building suffered at the hands of fanatical Moslems and from fire and was the subject of many additions and alterations.

When the Crusaders arrived from Europe on their mission to wrest the Holy Places from the Arabs at the end of the eleventh century they were dissatisfied with the size and appearance of the church and erected a larger and more pretentious edifice on its foundations. A hundred years later Saladin, the great Moslem commander, drove the Crusaders out of the Holy Land but he spared the church and kept the way open for Christian pilgrims to visit it. When the Ottoman Turks conquered Palestine early in the sixteenth century they also protected the church and maintained the right of pilgrimage.

In modern times the Church of the Holy Sepulchre has been subjected to almost every conceivable indignity. In 1808 it burned almost to the ground and a new building was constructed two years later. In 1834, at Easter time, it was the scene of a wild panic in which an eyewitness claimed that some four hundred worshipers were victims but his lurid account may be an exaggeration. In 1927 it was struck by an earthquake and its foundation and walls seriously weakened. In 1949 one dome was damaged by fire but was patched up. After the earthquake the British Mandate authorities, who had taken control of Palestine from the Turks during World War I, shored up the entrance facade of the church with an ugly skeleton of steel scaffolding for fear it would collapse on the heads of the pilgrims and placed a maze of wooden supports in the interior to keep it from falling apart. There it stood until seven years ago—shabby, neglected, and a peril to the faithful.

The principal reason that nothing was done to rehabilitate the Church of the Holy Sepulchre was the bitter rivalry—even warfare—that existed among the Christian sects accredited to it under a settlement known as the "Status Quo" proclaimed by the Turkish sultan in the nineteenth century.

On the very spot where Christ is believed to have died, this had taken the form of pitched battles with sticks, stones, bottles, fists, and harsh words between bands of monks, and it was one of the ostensible causes of the Crimean War. The controversy is a long, tortuous, and complicated one, with as many sides as there are contestants, but the chief adversaries are the Roman Catholics (Latins) and the Greek Orthodox (Greeks). The Latins and the Greeks traditionally have had the strongest claims to the Holy Sepulchre but they share these with the Armenians as representatives of the first country to accept Christianity. Over the centuries the Syrians, the Egyptian Copts and the black Abyssinians of Ethiopia have wangled tenuous footholds in the church, with the latter finally driven into a miserable tent on the roof.

In the preservation of their rights the dominant sects guard every square foot of their domain as though it were sovereign soil and patrol their boundaries as though they were political frontiers. Every floor, every wall, every cranny, and every object of worship is considered inviolate and the slightest infraction calls for retaliation. The keys to the Holy Sepulchre have always been treated as a symbol of this rivalry. At the time of his victory over the Crusaders, Saladin stipulated that these keys should always be held by a Moslem to prevent violence and preserve harmony. For nearly two hundred years this privilege has been exercised by two prominent families in Jerusalem: The Joudehs, who actually hold the keys, and the Nuseibehs, who actually lock and unlock the massive oaken doors. For a mere pittance they must be on the job seven days a week, for services of various kinds are held daily, and they are especially busy during Eastertide. The families also act as unofficial referees and try to keep the peace between the warring groups.

Such was the situation in 1959 when the Christians, prodded by the Jordan government, decided to close a shameful chapter and rebuild the church as a testament to the Master. Suppressing their jealousies, the Latins, Greeks, and Armenians pledged $2,000,000 to restore the structure to its twelfth century splendor and a ten-year task began. Each sect designated an architect to look out for its interests, accepted a joint superintendent, and set up a central Technical Bureau to referee disputes on a day-to-day basis. Working without a contractor, the Bureau supervises the execution of the work, allocates the jobs to be performed, buys the building materials and other supplies, and pays the staff and workmen, which number about fifty-five.

This is a delicate business and calls for a good measure of tact. The costs for the reconstruction of the Katholikon, the central nave of the church, for example, are borne by the Greeks, that of the chapels of Mary Magdalene and the Apparition and parts of the north transept by the Latins, and parts of the south transept by the Armenians in strict conformity with their rights, while those of the Rotunda and the Chapel of the Holy Sepulchre are charged to all three sects because they are held in common.

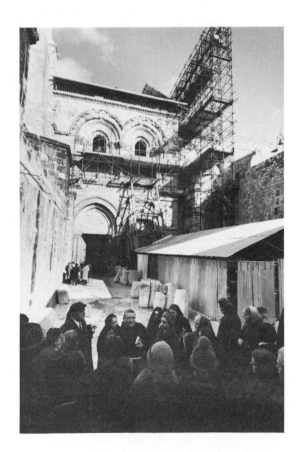

A group of pilgrims at the entrance to the Holy Sepulchre.

During the eras of Constantine and the Crusaders a white stone known as "Malaki" was used in the construction of the church and every effort is being made to supply this type from nearby quarries. The stone is brought to Jerusalem by truck, transferred to little handcarts, and carried through the narrow, cobbled streets of the Old City to the even narrower door of the basilica, some of the blocks weighing more than two thousand pounds. At night the debris is taken away on the backs of donkeys and over the past two years two thousand cubic meters of waste weighing some three thousand tons have been hauled away in this laborious manner.

If a visitor enters the square in front of the church these days he is greeted by the sound of hammers, chisels, and scrapers in the hands of swarthy Arab workers shaping up the stones while newly arrived blocks wait to be dressed. In one corner he sees a tin-roofed shed covering the stonemasons while they work, giving them protection against the sun in summer and the rain in winter. In another he watches a small hoist lifting the building materials to the rooftop as they are required and hauling down the rubble as it is disgorged. His eyes can make out the facade of the building only through a lattice-work of iron scaffolding, resembling the surgical dressings on the victim of an accident.

Inside the church the monks of the various communities perform their religious duties under a great strain while the reconstruction work goes on around them. They recite their prayers in makeshift chapels to the constant medley of noise and live their daily lives amid clouds

A choir in the courtyard of the Holy Sepulchre.

of dust. But the sacred life of the church goes on for pilgrims must be free to come and pray at the Holy Sepulchre and the building cannot be closed for a single day.

As of the time this book went to press, reconstruction of the dome, arches, and columns of the Greek Katholikon was well along and work was under way in the Latin chapels as well as parts of the north and south transepts. It is expected that the portion of the building dating to Crusader times will be completely restored by early 1967 and that the entire restoration will be finished by 1970. When the rusty steel scaffolding over the entrance comes down and the last wooden prop is removed from the interior, the Church of the Holy Sepulchre will again stand resplendent in Jerusalem the Golden, and Christians of all sects will be able, hopefully, to worship there again in the spirit of unity.

X

GIANT BUDDHAS:
PERILED BY ROCK
SLIDES

ᔕ ᔕ ᔕ

High on a cliff in northern Afghanistan two colossal,
rock-cut statues of Buddhist idols have looked out over
the Hindu Kush mountain range for at least thirteen
hundred years and probably longer. The taller of them,
the figure of a man, is 173 feet high or nearly three times
the height of the Abu Simbel statues in Nubia and the
Presidential busts on South Dakota's Mt. Rushmore, and
the shorter figure of a woman is 120 feet high. They
are mutilated relics of the days when the nearby city of
Bamian and its network of caves were one huge monastery
and shrine for pilgrims coming from all over Asia to kneel
before Guatama Buddha, the great teacher who lived five
hundred years before Christ. The taller one is probably

the largest replica of a human figure ever created by the hand of man.

The first recorded foreigner to set eyes on the idols was the famous Chinese traveler, Hsuan Tsang, who crossed the trackless Gobi Desert on foot, trudged through Turkestan in constant fear of his life from bandits and passed several days at Bamian on a pilgrimage to India in the seventh century. He found that the people of the valley were extremely devout and that their community harbored ten convents and about one thousand priests. His description of the statues in the authoritative *Buddhist Records of the Western World* is remarkably accurate on the whole: "To the North-east of the royal city there is a mountain, on the declivity of which is placed a stone figure of Buddha . . . Its golden hues sparkle on every side and its precious ornaments dazzle the eyes by their brightness. To the east of the convent there is a standing figure of Sakya Buddha, made of metallic stone (brass) . . . It has been cast in different parts and joined together, and thus placed in a completed form as it stands."

News of Hsuan's discovery slowly trickled into Europe and excited considerable interest. During the eighteenth and nineteenth centuries a number of European travelers visited the site and wrote about its wonders, some of their accounts being highly fanciful. At length Capt. M. G. Talbot, an engineer on the Africa Boundary Commission, made the first circumstantial report on the idols to the Royal Asiatic Society of Great Britain in 1886. Bamian, he noted, was situated in a small valley at a height of about 8,500 feet near the foot of the Koh-i-Baba mountain and about eighty miles from Kabul, the Afghan capital, on the main caravan road to Turkestan. Its history was obscure, he said, but it apparently had been a sacred city of Buddhist pilgrimage for many centuries until it was besieged and destroyed by Genghis Khan, the Mongol warlord, in 1222, and all its people slaughtered.

"But the most famous antiquities of Bamian," he wrote, "are certain standing figures of enormous size, carved in the conglomerate rock on the sides of the gorge. These images, which have been much injured by cannon shot, are cut in niches, both images and niches have been coated with plaster, whilst the plastered surface of the niches has been painted with figures. Bamian with its numerous grottos and with the singular red colour of its soil presents an impressive aspect of desolation and mystery."

Capt. Talbot measured the two Buddhas with scientific instruments for the first time and produced the measurements which are generally accepted today. The statues were draped in garments reaching to below the knee and were well executed in the Byzantine style. But their heads and faces had been disfigured and their arms, legs, and feet battered by sword thrusts or cannonballs at the hands of fanatical Moslems.

The idols were surrounded for six or seven miles on either side by a honeycomb of ancient caves hewn out of the face of the cliff and still used as dwellings and storehouses. Many of these were decorated with wall paintings and interconnected with steep, rambling passages and staircases cut in the rock. Up these staircases one could climb dangerously to the very heads of the statues. Peering down from this height the bystanders below looked like pygmies and their horses like dogs. Some idea of the size of the figures may be gained from the fact that their ears measured nine to twelve feet across and a man on horseback standing at their base did not reach as high as their toes.

When UNESCO dispatched a mission to Bamian in May, 1962, they found that the Buddhas were threatened by falling rock from above and by the deterioration of the cliff face generally. A huge slab of rock three thousand tons in weight was in danger of collapsing and crashing down on the idols. Rivulets of water dripping down from the peak of the cliff were cutting troughs in the stone and creating cracks which weakened the wall. When two vertical cracks met with a horizontal one it had the effect of isolating an entire block of rock and causing it to cave in.

The archaeologists estimated that the face of the cliff had receded some thirty or more feet over the centuries as a result of water seepage, weathering, and sharp temperature changes, and predicted it would continue at an accelerated rate if nothing were done to stop it. They discovered that a double brick buttress had been built against the cliff between the statues about twenty years ago by the Afghan Direction of Antiquities to prevent the rock slide and some work had been done to divert the dripping water, but the effort was insufficient and the buttress itself had developed a deep crevice and cracked open.

The taller of the two immense statues of Buddhist idols at Bamian.

Dismissing the idea of reinforcing the buttress and suggesting that it be eliminated entirely, they proposed to restore the original facade of the cliff by constructing an internal support to hold up the section of rock endangered by the most serious crack, and to rebuild the face of the wall to hide the support. This would be accomplished in seven steps: 1. Separate the base of the buttress from the wall. 2. Erect two banks of temporary props to support the buttress during the work. 3. Recement the major crack in the wall. 4. Remove the rock below the crack piece by piece. 5. Rebuild a three-foot wall of masonry against the face of the cliff. 6. To build the wall place stone blocks side by side and join them with cement or concrete. 7. Destroy the buttress and leave only the new support. Most of this work would revolve around the small Buddha, which is the more seriously threatened, but similar repairs would be made to the Great Buddha. To render the monuments more available to the public the mission recommended construction of a new access road leading out of the main east-west highway from Kabul and a shorter road at the base of the cliff connecting the two Buddhas to permit direct passage.

If the funds are available and the forces of nature in the form of rock and water are stayed from destruction, twentieth-century pilgrims flying in to Afghanistan by modern jets may be able in the not too distant future to tread in the footsteps of Hsuan Tsang and gaze upon the faces of the Buddhist idols almost exactly as he saw them thirteen centuries ago.

XI

MOHENJO-DARO: MENACED BY SALT WATER

⊄ ⊄ ⊄

Nearly two hundred miles north of the port of Karachi in West Pakistan lie the vast ruins of Mohenjo-Daro (Mound of the Dead) and the Indus Valley civilization, one of the world's earliest and greatest.

Unknown to archaeologists until its accidental discovery about forty years ago, the relics of Mohenjo-Daro sprawl across 250 acres of desert near the banks of the Indus River and still bear evidence of a rich culture that flourished between 4000 and 2000 B.C., contemporary with that of Sumeria and Egypt. When the British authorities were building a railway line in 1922 they noticed that an unusual amount of burnt brick was available in the area and their curiosity led them to the uncovering of the dead city or rather half-a-dozen cities piled one on top of the other.

Successive excavation brought to light a remarkable complex of shops and homes, bathhouses and theaters, streets and walls indicative of a high standard of life. Among the artifacts found were engraved seals, tools, weapons, jewelry, sculpture, and pottery of a high order of design and workmanship. Despite intensive research, little is known about the people of the City of the Dead to this day—their race, religion, origin, or fate—except that they may have been engulfed by the Aryan invasion of India about two thousand years before Christ.

However, a joint expedition of the University of Pennsylvania Museum and the Pakistan Archaeological Department cast considerable doubt on the invasion theory. The scientists uncovered a massive brick barrier surrounding one part of Mohenjo-Daro, more than twenty feet deep, which they decided could not have been intended for military defense and must have been erected as a protection against flooding from the Indus River. They also found the remains of five skeletons buried in a pile of debris but there was no evidence that they had met a violent end.

They came to the tentative conclusion that a series of geological upheavals had split the earth south of the city toward the peak of its existence and had formed a gigantic lake from the waters of the Indus, enveloping the city. Apparently the city was gradually subjected to floods over a period of time, perhaps as much as a hundred years, which gave the authorities plenty of opportunity to throw up protective embankments such as the one found. But the barriers failed to hold back the waters in the end, parts of the city were abandoned from time to time, and some of the people fled. Finally a mountain of mud descended on the place and engulfed it, snuffing out the lives of the remaining residents. The archaeologists emphasize that this hypothesis requires further study before the fate of Mohenjo-Daro can be definitely settled.

It was obvious, at any rate, that Mohenjo-Daro was a great trade center at the peak of its prosperity, due to its strategic position on the Indus. The city was well built, even by modern town-planning standards. Most of the streets were very narrow to offer protection against the sun but the main arteries in the center were as broad as modern boulevards. The principal building material used was brick made of baked red clay, as stone and wood were

A section of the brick-laid drainage system running through the city at Mohenjo-Daro.

extremely scarce, and the bricks were held together by a type of mortar. This permitted the construction of multiple-story dwellings and shops in a highly congested community.

To bring in water and take out waste, the city authorities installed a complicated network of canals, underground pipes and sewers which are described as among the most ingenious of ancient times. The water was brought in along the canals and piped into small wells inside the houses. If the sewers got clogged up they could be cleared by emptying shallow draining wells into them. The more prosperous residents enjoyed bathrooms within their homes and the rest had access to public bathing establishments. Long before the Romans, the public baths were the center of social life for much of the city.

The material comforts of such social life were judged in part by the artifacts uncovered. These include a few examples of Indus sculpture such as the stone statue of a husky man with a heavy face and slanting eyes wearing a decorative cloak and the bronze figurine of a dancing girl with her arms adorned with bangles from wrist to shoulder. Other indications may be found in art objects exquisitely fashioned from gold, silver, bronze, copper, and tin imported from afar and in jewelry skillfully fitted with precious and semi-precious stones.

Some clues to the religion of Mohenjo-Daro were extracted from the engraved seals left behind. Some of these depict bulls, monkeys, tigers, and elephants surrounding a Deity with his arms covered with bracelets and two horns on his head: The Horned God. Others show the

Part of the staircase leading to the upper storey of a house in Mohenjo-Daro.

Circular wells reaching as high as the second floors of the buildings were common in Mohenjo-Daro.

An underground canal which brought fresh water into the city.

A round well found in one of the houses of Mohenjo-Daro.

The public baths.

animals in the presence of a female Deity, or Horned Goddess. Outside of these fragments little is known about the strange cult. Long before Alexander the Great passed that way in the fourth century B.C. to achieve the conquest of India, the Gods of Mohenjo-Daro had been toppled, its people had disappeared, and it was truly a City of the Dead. So it exists today and most of its secrets remain to be unlocked by the spades of future archaeologists.

When UNESCO sent a mission of three experts to Mohenjo-Daro in January, 1964, to investigate the condition of the ruins, they found that most of them had been covered with deposits of mineral salts from the flooding of the Indus River and these were eating away the bricks at an alarming rate as a result of capillary action. (The chemical attraction between a liquid and a solid.) They described the scene as looking like a field of snow.

"Glassy needles a centimeter in length sprouted from shady walls," they reported, "and, where the ground was rough and exposed to the direct action of the sun, the salt formed a white cushion—like masses pressing upwards as in a vegetable garden well stocked with cauliflowers."

The mission reached the immediate conclusion that the only practical way of disposing of this great mass of saline material was to redissolve it and return it to the Indus by pumping the liquid into the ancient drainage system. In preparation for this task they drafted a large contour map of the area with aerial and ground photographs and accumulated a body of information from an analysis of soil, salt, and water as to the nature of the subsurface geology. On the basis of this data they were able to plan the locations of their drainage outlets and the distribution of their pumping equipment.

As a more permanent solution, the experts thought it was possible to lower the water table in the area but this would leave a vast quantity of salt behind where the water receded. This, too, would have to be dissolved and fed back into the river through a network of strategically placed drains. With an annual rainfall of only about three inches, it would take considerable time to clear the ground completely of its salty curse.

To halt the erosion of the bricks they decided there were several supplementary steps that could be taken: 1. The underground water must be removed by pumping or drainage. 2. Areas alongside walls must be cleaned to stop salty water from infiltrating through the surrounding earth and debris. 3. The walls must be cleared regularly of salts and dust borne by the winds and pounded in by rainfall. 4. The brick must be leached with fresh water to extract the salt.

Additional studies are being made to arrive at a more detailed program of conservation but whatever is done it will be a long and costly business to save the remains of Mohenjo-Daro. If it is not carried out the ruins may be totally destroyed within a few decades by the action of the salt. If it is, the City of the Dead may rise again, archaeologically speaking, and stand indefinitely as a monument to the great civilization of the Indus Valley.

Although it is in an extremely remote area, the Pakistan authorities have taken several measures to make Mohenjo-Daro accessible to the public. An airstrip capable of taking light planes has been laid down near the entrance to the excavation and a concrete road built to the nearest railroad station. The site has been laced with asphalt roads and brick footpaths and staircases have been installed. A modern rest house, a small museum, and a little mosque have been added to accommodate foreign and native visitors.

XII

ANGKOR: SNATCHED

FROM THE JUNGLE

⊂ ⊂ ⊂

Deep in the jungles of northern Cambodia, the mighty rulers of the Khmer Empire carved out a great, sprawling capital in stone from the ninth to the fifteenth centuries. Greatest of all their monuments was Angkor Wat, the sacred temple-tomb of their most illustrious monarch. No less impressive was Angkor Thom, a complex of structures forming the city proper. Between them were a hundred or more palaces, theaters, shrines, and other buildings reflecting the opulence of a rich civilization. The fantastic creation as a whole has come to be known as Angkor, the lost city of the jungle.

The Khmers apparently were an amalgam of the original Cambodians and conquering Hindus from South India. Their religion was a blend of various forms of Buddhism and Hinduism. Their culture was characterized by a high order of art and architecture. At the pinnacle of their power they wrought the most brilliant civilization in Southeast Asia.

In the twelfth century King Suryavarman II erected in the Mekong River Valley the colossal temple of Angkor Wat (City Temple) as a replica of the mythical Mount Meru, home of the gods. It is approached by a quarter-mile long causeway crossing a 200-yard moat and sits in the middle of a rectangular park almost a mile long.

The main edifice rises in three stages connected by ex-

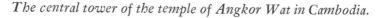

The central tower of the temple of Angkor Wat in Cambodia.

The south gallery of Angkor Wat.

terior staircases. It culminates in the Holy Sanctuary with a series of towers, the tallest of which is 215 feet high. The central block is about 650 feet square and is surrounded by a continuous gallery·formed by a row of pillars on the outer side and a solid wall on the inner side. On the inner wall is carved an extraordinary panel of bas-reliefs 2,600 feet long, extending from floor to ceiling, which depict in the minutest detail the interaction of gods, men, and animals in the Hindu legend of the Churning of the Milky Sea, a subtle, complex story symbolic of the unending struggle between good and evil.

Half a century later, the next ruler, King Jayavarman

VII, the most prolific of all the Khmer builders, created the walled city of Angkor Thom (Great City) in the form of a square two miles long on each side and entered by five enormous gates. Its most imposing structure was the Bayon, a pyramid-type temple with a double system of galleries, a huge central tower rising from a circular base and fifty-four small towers decorated with two hundred faces of a Hindu god. Nearby were the Royal Palace, the Terrace of the Leper King, and the Elephants' Terrace. Outside the walls were three other impressive shrines. Within and without the walls were grotesque stone figures of elephants and serpents, Titans and Gods pictured in the struggle of the Churning of the Milky

The Eastern Gate, or Gate of Victory, of the Royal Palace at Angkor Thom.

A partial view of the Elephants' Terrace at Angkor Thom.

Sea. Some authorities regard Angkor Thom as the largest city in the world of its time with a million or more inhabitants living a life of luxury. Its wealth was based on rice and the cultivation of the crop required an extensive system of dikes, reservoirs, and canals for irrigation purposes.

After the death of King Jayavarman early in the thirteenth century, Angkor lost its dynamic qualities and began to go downhill but it clung to its faded glory for another two centuries. Towards the middle of the fifteenth century the Siamese ravaged the countryside, pillaged the capital, and toppled the reigning dynasty. The conquerors deported masses of the population and others fled to more peaceful surroundings. The vast irrigation system fell into disrepair and the production of rice dwindled. Slowly but inexorably the green jungle swallowed up the capital and its temples and Ankgor almost vanished from the pages of history for four hundred years.

In 1861 Henri Mouhot, a French naturalist, stumbled into a clearing while hacking his way through the rain forests of Cambodia and cast his eyes on an enormous stone structure lighted by a reddish glow from the sun. He gasped as he realized that the tales spun by Portuguese and Spanish explorers were true: This was the long-lost city of Angkor. During the ensuing days he uncovered scores of other temples half-strangled by the jungle growths and he wrote in his journal that here were "perhaps the grandest, the most important and the most artistically perfect monuments the past has left to us."

About this time France established a protectorate over Cambodia as part of its Indo-Chinese empire and began to send scientific expeditions to Angkor. In 1907 Angkor was taken from Siam and restored to Cambodia. In the same year the Angkor Conservatory was set up in Paris and the serious work of clearing, maintaining, restoring, and sometimes reconstructing the ruins was begun.

When the first French archaeologist descended on the scene he found that the jungle had engulfed all the temples and they were in ruins with the exception of Angkor Wat which was badly dilapidated. The roots of giant bombax and banyan trees had wrapped their tentacles around the monuments, pried roofs and walls apart, and split statuary in two as with a mailed fist. Huge vines had crept insidiously into crevices in the stones and covered gates, terraces and sculptured idols with a thick matting that almost hid them from view. It was an eerie place of solitude with no humans in sight and only the sounds of wild beasts, birds, and bats to break the silence.

The archaeologist and his helpers labored for three years just to push the jungle back beyond the immediate precincts of Angkor. When all the growth had been cleared away he set about repairing the stonework of the temples of Angkor Wat and restoring it to some semblance of its former splendor. He worked with a small band of peasants in intense tropical heat and under pelting rains with the threat of bandits always in the offing.

From Angkor Wat the archaeologist turned to Angkor Thom and its palaces. Here the jungle had overpowered everything and there was little left of the Bayon Temple and the Royal Palace except heaps of stones and rotted timbers lying on the ground. He cleared the sites, traced the foundations, and carried out some excavations preliminary to the work of actual restoration.

The next man on the job was an architect and he applied architectural methods to the problem. He used reinforced concrete to strengthen many of the temples and he was so successful that they emerged stronger than they had been in their prime. He also adapted a Greek technique called anastylosis, employed on the Acropolis, to

A view of the Bayon Temple at Angkor Thom showing the faces of the god on the fronts of the towers.

A detail of one of the faces on the towers of Bayon Temple.

dismantle a building stone by stone, match them up on the ground with fallen stones, and reassemble them as a whole exactly as they once stood.

In recent years the government of independent Cambodia has displayed an interest in this work by allocating funds. Virtually all the temples have been stripped of vegetation and restored at least in part with the exception of one which has deliberately been left as it was, with trees and vines throttling it in a deadly embrace to show visitors the power of the jungle. Even today during the rainy season a small army of workmen is kept busy eradicating jungle growths in an unceasing conflict of art against nature. Like that of a housewife, an archaeologist's work apparently is never done.

Once the temples had been freed from the jungle other problems arose to plague the archaeologists. Protected in part by the very vegetation that had strangled them for centuries, the temples were now exposed to the searing heat, high humidity, and torrential rains of Cambodia. In addition, some stones were attacked by bacteria, others by lichen and still others by a variety of "stone diseases." In some cases, whole groups of statuary had tumbled into the water and entire staircases had crumbled into rubble. The task of resurrecting the lost city of Angkor continues to this day and literally will never be finished but already modern technicians have accomplished feats of reconstruction worthy of the ancient kings of Khmer.

XIII

WHITE HERON CASTLE: REBUILT IN BEAUTY

⊏⊨ ⊏⊨ ⊏⊨

During the feudal period in Japan from about the twelfth to the mid-nineteenth centuries the castle was the back-bone of the ruling system and it has been estimated that there were more than five thousand of them dotted about the land at one time. Japanese castles were built by war-lords primarily as military strongholds in the incessant wars they fought among themselves but their location was selected partly on the basis of scenic advantages and their design partly on architectural beauty. After the downfall of the Shoguns and the restoration of the Meiji Dynasty in 1868, castles lost their reason for existence with the end of the feudal system, and the government ordered their destruction. But some were spared and to-day there are twenty-seven castles left, of which five are classified as national treasures. Among these the greatest

and most beautiful is White Heron Castle or Hakuro-Jo
as it is known in Japanese.

The origins of the White Heron go back to the fourteenth century when a local warlord built a fortress on a
hill overlooking the town of Himeji in the south as a base
for an attack on the Ashigaga Shoguns in Kyoto. Three
hundred years later a six-story tower was added to the
structure and it commanded the countryside for miles
around. For the next two and a half centuries the castle
played a small role in one of the most peaceful periods
in Japanese history, and its last owners lived there for
ten generations. During the Second World War it was a
military headquarters but emerged unscathed despite the
heavy bombardment of nearby Himeji by the U. S. Air
Force.

Like all Japanese castles the White Heron was formed
of moats, drawbridges, walls, and gates but it is one of the
few examples left of the spiral type of defense. That is,
the lines of defense were so laid out that the attacking
forces could be confronted and ambushed at a number of
places and by a number of means. If the attackers broke
through the main gate they could be met by a counter-
attack in the interior and perhaps driven into the moat. If
this failed the besiegers had to penetrate a maze of additional gates and walls, pitfalls and labyrinths before they
could reach the principal keep where the commander and
the bulk of his troops were stationed. As they pressed the
attack they were met by a hail of bullets, arrows, and
rocks from overhanging walls, niches, and portholes. As
originally built, the castle was equipped with about six

hundred portholes for archers and about twenty-five hundred for musketeers.

As seen today, the White Heron tower is about one hundred feet high and has a total floor area of about three thousand square yards. The main building is composed of one major tower-keep and three minor keeps, connected with one another by a series of bridges, each of which forms a small inner court. Topped by a heavy roof, the

The tower of the White Heron Castle in Japan.

The White Heron Castle.

main tower is estimated to weigh about six thousand tons and this entire weight is supported by two king posts about forty inches in diameter which extend throughout the structure. The castle was designed not only as a stronghold but it embraced a commodious residence for the vassal of the reigning warlord, including a "boudoir tower" for his consort and a rare "powder room." With its copper-rusted roof, its tier on tier of ornamental gables, and its gleaming white walls, the White Heron stands out as the most striking landmark for visitors coming from Kobe.

Although the castle escaped war damage, it had suffered serious deterioration over the centuries as a result of assaults and fire and it became the first state-owned castle to be restored with state funds. After an initial attempt before the war the work of rebuilding it was resumed in 1956 and completed in 1964. The latter required nearly $1,500,000 and 200,000 man-days of labor and was overseen by the National Commission for the Protection of Cultural Properties.

When the engineers came to inspect the structure they found that the ground under the tower had sunk, like that of Pisa, causing it to lean nine inches out of line at the top, that the cantilevers supporting the tile roofs had been weakened, and that the roofs themselves had sagged badly. They decided the tower must be completely overhauled by dismantling and reassembling it and called on many devices and techniques of modern engineering and architecture to do the job.

As the first step, a reinforced concrete frame measuring eighteen by thirty-six feet was lowered onto the bedrock ten feet below the surface and the king posts, which were still structurally sound, were re-erected on this foundation. When it came time to reassemble the wooden framework of the tower, steel wire was used where stresses were expected to be unusually strong to make it sturdier and sag-proof.

As to the walls, the architects developed a new type of mortar to replace the original and applied seven or eight coatings to cover a surface of about 27,000 square yards. This resulted in a wall thickness varying from thirteen to thirty-nine inches and walls that are expected to last for two hundred years.

Moving to the roof, they replaced 85 per cent of the tiles on the main keep with newly baked tiles and about the same percentage on the three adjoining turrets, using 130,000 new tiles in all. In laying the tiles they eliminated the customary use of mud and affixed them directly to the wooden base, making the new roof 550 tons lighter than the old one.

In reconstructing the castle, the contractors were careful to preserve the taper of its tower, recognizing that it is considered the most nearly perfect in all Japan. (If the rate of tapering is too great it might be more stable but less attractive.) As completed, the topmost floor still has an area 21 per cent less than that of the lowest floor and the same proportion remains in the middle floors. The degree of inclination of the roof also varies from floor to floor, the angle of the highest being larger than the one below it and so on down to the bottom.

When the task was finished, connoisseurs of Japanese castles rejoiced that it looked almost exactly as it did three hundred and fifty years ago. Once more it stood proudly as an almost impregnable fortress capable of withstanding the onslaughts of its enemies, demonstrating the prestige of its master and, at the same time, evoking the admiration of its friends as a thing of beauty. No longer must it stand off the rival warlords of feudal times but it must contend with the invasion of the modern tourist hordes, awing them with its might and inspiring them with its artistry.

XIV

EMPRESS CATHERINE'S
PALACE: REDEEMED
FROM WAR

⊏⊐ ⊏⊐ ⊏⊐

Peter the Great of Russia created the little town of Tsarkoye Selo (Tsar's Village) near St. Petersburg early in
the eighteenth century as a country estate for his wife
Catherine the First. Towards the middle of the century
his daughter, Empress Elizabeth, built a magnificent palace there and it became the summer residence of the Romanoff Dynasty for more than one hundred and fifty
years. When the formidable Catherine the Great came to
power later in the century she reconstructed and enlarged
the palace and the town became a health resort. In 1837
the first Russian railroad was laid out to connect it with
St. Petersburg, fifteen miles to the north, and in 1887
Tsarkoye Selo became the first community in Europe—if

not the world—to be entirely lighted by electricity. With or without lights, Empress Catherine's palace has competed with Peter's Grand Palace in nearby Peterhof ever since for the title of the Russian Versailles.

After several Russian architects had started construction, Elizabeth engaged Count V. V. Rastrelli, son of an Italian sculptor who had settled in the country, to remold the palace in the baroque style so popular in Europe at the time and give her something to rival the most brilliant creations of the French Court, which had been slavishly admired by her father. Rastrelli spared neither money, materials, nor serf labor to satisfy his patron. He erected a three-story structure about one thousand feet long and nearly seventy feet high occupying seven thousand square feet of ground, and decorated it inside and out with a lavish hand—not always in good taste by modern standards. Its central feature was the Throne Room or Great Hall which was more than two hundred feet long and covered 1600 square yards. Its walls were lined with mirrors, as in Versailles, and faced with fifty windows in two tiers, offering an illusion of limitless space. Its floors were inlaid with precious woods in the shape of rays radiating from a central sun. Its lofty ceiling was painted with ornate figures of goddesses, angels, and cupids so beloved of the times. Nearly every foot of it was adorned with gaudy fretwork in the form of garlands of flowers, leaves, and curlicues.

Leading into the Throne Room was an elegant hallway stretching the length of the building and flanked with a series of reception rooms, salons, and dining rooms on either side. One of these was the Picture Hall which was covered solidly with the canvases of the European masters. Another was the Amber Room which was fashioned out of a huge panel of amber presented to Peter by King Frederick I of Prussia as a diplomatic gesture. (In return the Tsar sent Frederick fifty-five of his tallest soldiers to serve in his bodyguard.) At one end was a small church as richly designed as the other rooms for court services. Almost everything was embellished with heavy layers of gold and silver, precious and semi-precious stones. About 220 pounds of pure gold went into the decoration. The job took four years to complete and required several thousand serfs laboring for a pittance.

The Picture Hall of Empress Catherine's palace after restoration.

On her accession to the throne Catherine II hired Charles Cameron, a Scottish architect who detested the baroque motif, to remodel and enlarge the palace and he introduced the classic style, retaining Rastrelli's work in the central halls but drastically altering the northern and southern wings. He added the so-called Cameron Gallery with its graceful pillars, the Green Dining Room, Blue Reception Room, the Chinese Drawing Room, and he built private apartments for Catherine and her son Paul.

The Green Dining Room as it was restored.

The Chinese Drawing Room after restoration.

Among the latter was the Silver Study from which the aging Empress, shrewd and strong-willed, directed the affairs of her empire. Cameron also laid out a 720-acre park in front of the palace with rare trees, shrubs, and flowers, lakes and streams, pavilions and kiosks, creating a sylvan retreat.

Some idea of the pomp and ceremony enfolding the Catherine Palace may be gleaned from a contemporary writer's description of a reception given by the Empress at the time: "Distinguished guests of both sexes thronged the apartments of the palace in resplendent attire and jewels. Suddenly the curtain fell and there was darkness, immediately followed by the light of a thousand and 200 candles reflected in the mirrors. A band of 60 musicians started up and the ball began. The first steps of the minuet were interrupted by a muffled clamor. The doors were flung open and the Empress was beheld seated on a gorgeous throne. She descended and entered the big hall surrounded by a ring of brilliant courtiers."

After the October Revolution of 1917 all this came to an end and Tsar Nicholas II, last of the Romanoff's, and his family were imprisoned at Tsarkoye Selo for several months before they were sent eastward to their deaths. Shortly after this the name of the town was changed to Dyetskoye Selo (Children's Village), the palace was turned into a museum, and other buildings were converted into schools, hospitals, and rest homes for children. Still later the town was renamed Pushkin in honor of the illustrious Russian poet, Alexander Pushkin, who went to school there as a boy early in the nineteenth century. A small wooden house and a statue still stand to his memory.

Two years after the outbreak of the Second World War Pushkin was occupied by German forces for three years (1941-1944) during the siege of Leningrad (formerly St. Petersburg), and the Catherine Palace and park were heavily damaged. Some of the damage was apparently due to military action—bombing and shelling—and

The facade of The Catherine Palace as it looked in 1944 after being wrecked by the Germans.

some to wanton vandalism. Nazi troops used the palace as a barracks and they almost completely wrecked it as soldiers have done throughout history. Although the bulk of the art collection had been evacuated for safe-keeping, the invaders smashed hundreds of mirrors in the Throne Room, shattered statuary, defaced the paintings that were left and stole everything they could lay their hands on, according to Russian sources. As part of the loot, the priceless panels were stripped from the Amber Room and spirited back to Germany where they disappeared in one of the great art mysteries of the war. On top of this much of the palace was destroyed in a fire in 1942.

When the siege of Leningrad lifted in early 1944 and the Germans were forced to surrender Pushkin they planted time bombs inside the palace on the eve of their withdrawal with the intention of blowing up what was left of it. But Soviet mine engineers discovered and disarmed eleven of them before they exploded. As the defenders moved back in they found that the palace was largely a blackened shell and its remaining treasures were a heap of debris. Thousands of pieces of torn pictures, broken sculptures, cracked furniture, and sawed-off works of art were scattered around the grounds and along the line of retreat. The park was mined and crisscrossed with barbed wire and many of the trees had been cut down. The Pushkin statue was riddled with bullets in what appeared to be a last futile act of retaliation.

Beginning in 1957 and continuing to the present the enormous task of reconstructing the Catherine Palace went forward feverishly under the direction of the Pushkin Municipal Council and the State Inspection Service for the Preservation of Monuments. First of all the facade of the building was restored to its eighteenth century condition and the opportunity was seized to replace a large balcony which had been added in the nineteenth century as a distortion, with one more in line with Rastrelli's design. Throughout the project a policy of correcting de-

The facade of the palace as it is today, after restoration.

partures from the original architects' plans was carried out.

As the contractors advanced into the interior they discovered that the Throne Room had not been seriously affected by the 1942 fire but the old wooden rafters had been damaged by artillery shells and had to be replaced. They solved this by a uniquely modern method involving the use of a helicopter. Over a period of six hours the "copter" slipped through the open roof time after time, with its huge rotor blades fanning the air, to lift out thirty-one slabs of oak weighing over two tons each and to deposit eleven lighter metal girders in their place.

Concentrating on the least damaged sections, the workmen repaired the main staircase leading to the second floor, which was a mass of rubble, the palace church, and thirteen rooms in the northern part of the building. These included the Picture Hall, part of the Empress' apartments, the Green Dining Room, the Chinese Drawing Room, and the Blue Reception Room. When this area had been restored all the treasures which had been hidden in the countryside at the outset of the conflict—paintings, sculptures, furniture, chinaware, glassware, and bronzes—were brought back on a memorable day of triumph and reinstalled in their rightful places as part of an exhibition.

The top of the main staircase of the palace after being repaired.

The restoration of other works of art which had remained in the palace presented a knottier problem. The archives, libraries, and museums of Leningrad and other cities were ransacked for old photographs, drawings, water colors, and documents of the eighteenth century and examined for clues which would guide the reconstruction of the wreckage with scientific accuracy. Master craftsmen and talented young specialists, many of whom had been trained in the Leningrad High School of Applied Arts, were enlisted to re-create the originals in the most faithful detail and with loving care. The Soviet government allocated special funds for this work and made available scarce materials such as gold leaf, colored woods, and rare paints.

The Blue Reception Room, the largest and most attractive one to be rehabilitated, is a good example of the painstaking nature of this work. Its former brilliance in paint and gilt, carvings and moldings, woods and silks, mirrors and marble was recaptured out of broken fragments, intensive research and imagination. Its blue silks with printed floral designs were duplicated in a Moscow factory from old specimens with the advice of the Silk Research Institute. Damaged scraps were pieced together to rebuild doors, mirror frames, fireplaces, and a plastic frieze. The ceiling was redecorated precisely as of old from drawings left by the architect Cameron. New furniture, vases, and floor lamps made of blue glass and crystal were built out of the wrecks of the old and installed in their proper places.

While much remains to be done before the Catherine

The Blue Reception Room after being restored.

Palace stands complete in its eighteenth century grandeur, its present state of restoration is a source of swelling pride to the Soviet people. More than 2,000,000 visitors, including foreigners from thirty countries, have gazed on its wonders since the museum reopened in 1959. When it is finally finished it will truly be a monument to man's capacity to devote the arts of peace to mending the ravages of war.

XV

UNITED STATES CAPITOL: THREATENED WITH COLLAPSE

⊑ ⊑ ⊑

The United States Capitol is not an antiquity in terms of the preceding edifices but, together with the White House, it is the oldest public building in Washington, D.C. and the danger of its collapsing from old age is exceeded by no other structure on earth. The East Wing of the stately, 166-year-old edifice was constructed and enlarged five years ago at a cost of $24,000,000 but the West Wing, looking out over Constitution Mall and the Washington Monument, is in even greater, more imminent peril and the price of its salvation may run to $34,-000,000.

President George Washington laid the cornerstone of the Capitol in September, 1793, on Jenkins Hill in ac-

cordance with the master plan envisioned by Major
Pierre Charles L'Enfant, a French architect, for the construction of the new city and with a design drawn up by
Dr. William Thornton, a physician, but professional architects were brought in later. His design was the win-
ner of a $500 contest and President Washington approved
it as having "grandeur, simplicity, and convenience." It
called for a simple one-story building in a mixed Greek-
Renaissance style.

Rising eighty-eight feet above the Potomac River on
a remote, wooded site of four acres, the first Capitol was
planned as an almost square structure with a central
domed section of Virginia sandstone and two wings of
white Massachusetts marble to accommodate the House
of Representatives and the Senate. The northern or Senate Wing was completed first and it was here that President John Adams addressed the first joint session of Congress in November, 1800, commenting in passing "on the
prospect of a residence not to be changed." The Supreme
Court and other departments of government crowded in
a year later and the southern wing was close enough to
completion for the House to occupy it in 1807.

During the War of 1812 the British set fire to the Capitol, along with the White House, and burned out the interior, leaving it in ruins. For five years Congress legis-
lated without a permanent home until two architects,
Benjamin H. Latrobe and Charles Bulfinch, rebuilt the
building, and Congress reoccupied it in 1819. Ten years
later the East Front was added and was used for the in-
auguration of President Andrew Jackson.

The Capitol as we know it today was greatly enlarged beginning in 1851 as President Millard Fillmore laid the cornerstone, and Daniel Webster made the oration, and ending during the Civil War with the addition of the Senate Chamber and the Hall of Representatives. With this enlargement, the building measured 751 feet long, 350 feet wide, and 307 feet high from its base to the tip of the colossal Statue of Freedom atop the dome. Within its walls are 533 rooms devoted to legislative functions, many of them embellished with historic paintings and statuary.

About the same time, the original dome was replaced by the present huge dome, made of pre-shaped wedges of cast iron, over the rotunda. As the capital's most prominent landmark, it has 108 windows and 365 steps from bottom to top but it has long been closed to the public. At the top of the dome a striking fresco painted by Constantino Brumidi, an Italian immigrant, depicts the strength of the Union in bigger-than-life figures under the motto: *E Pluribus Unum* ("Out of many, one"). Along its rim runs a 300-foot frieze portraying American history from Christopher Columbus in 1492 to the Wright Brothers in 1903 as painted by Brumidi and others. The Statue of Freedom above is made of bronze, is 19½ feet tall and weighs about fifteen thousand pounds.

Next to the White House, the Capitol is the most popular sight in Washington with more than 5,000,000 visitors a year trooping through its halls to see where the nation's laws are made. Many of them listen to debates in the House and Senate, visit Statuary Hall where eighty-six

The West Wing of the United States Capitol building.

statues of statesmen from forty-seven states are on display, tarry in the rotunda beneath the dome to admire four historical masterpieces, or pause in the Nonsectarian Room for Meditation for a moment of silent prayer. For this truly belongs to all the people in a self-governing democracy.

It was thus a question of national concern some years ago when it was revealed that the East Front of the Capitol was in danger of collapse. Despite loud protests from purists, the facade was extended 32½ feet, the crumbling sandstone walls were duplicated in marble and additional space to make 102 new rooms was gained but the old outside walls were preserved within the interior. The work took three years and was apparently worthwhile judging by the public's reception.

Large cracks above a window in the West Wall of the Capitol building.

No sooner was this accomplished than it was found that the West Front was in an even more precarious position and there was a real threat that the massive dome might crash in on the heads of the visitors. After several years of fruitless wrangling the problem was presented to a Commission of the 89th Congress in the summer of 1965. The testimony of the engineering experts at the hearing was hair-raising by any standard.

With Vice-President Hubert H. Humphrey sitting in, Dr. Miles N. Clair, president of a seventy-year-old engineering firm in Brookline, Massachusetts, which had been retained to make a study of the problem, sketched a disturbing picture of the disintegration of the West Central section of the Capitol. He pointed out that no professional architect or engineer, except for President Washington, had a hand in the original construction of the building and that the builders were handicapped by their limited knowledge of the subject, the scarcity of materials, and the lack of skilled craftsmen. After the British bonfire, the architects engaged to reconstruct the edifice got embroiled in a dispute with the Congressional Committee in charge—then as now—and walked off the job with the original plans in their pocket, depriving their successors of much pertinent information.

Starting from the ground up, the witness testified that the foundation soil under some sections of the structure was not able to bear the burden placed on it and this had caused the building to shift its position. This movement had produced gaping cracks in the walls extending all the way down through the structure. At the same time, he

Fissures in the West Wall of the Capitol building.

continued, the sandstone in the exterior wall had seriously deteriorated and the stone lintels and keystones had slipped downward—so badly in some cases that the windows could hardly be opened. If nothing was done to correct the situation, the witness predicted it would eventually result in a partial collapse of the building and when he was asked to define "eventually," he snapped: "This is not a matter of five years. This is a matter of now."

At another point in his testimony, Dr. Clair pointed to one wall in a photograph and stated flatly, "This wall is about to fall down," and when the Committee asked what would happen in that event he retorted, "Somebody might be killed." The most critical areas demanding immediate attention, he said, were the entablature (the wall supporting the roof), the wall at the terrace level on the old Senate Wing and the corresponding wall on the old House Wing, and these required emergency action "Immediately." When pushed to say what he meant by that the witness replied: "Next week. I am not kidding. I think it is so serious something should be done at once."

But such stopgap measures would only put off the evil day, the engineer went on, and the rehabilitation job should be done as a whole at the earliest possible time as was done on the East Wing. He referred to fears that a minor earthquake somewhere in the vicinity or even an airplane crash nearby might spell danger and warned that they could cause partial or total collapse of the structure's stones and walls.

At this juncture Speaker of the House, John W. Mc-Cormack, Chairman of the Commission, cited the fact that the architect of the Capitol, J. George Stewart, had recommended adoption of the Clair report and called for action. "We are faced with a very serious situation," he said. "If anything should happen the responsibility rests on the members of the Commission." With Vice-President Humphrey and Republican Minority Leader, Gerald R. Ford in support, the Commission unanimously accepted the report and the first step was taken to meet the crisis.

The architect of the Capitol was then authorized to submit to the Senate and House Appropriation Committee a request for $300,000 to pay for the cost of drafting preliminary plans and estimates for the extension of the West Wing and there the matter rests. At a subsequent meeting the Commission directed that emergency steps be taken to shore up the most critical sections with heavy timbers and this work was executed out of an existing appropriation later in the year.

Whether Congress will rise to the occasion and complete the preservation of the Capitol is a question that was embroiled in a heated controversy as this book went to press. Washington observers recall that Congress authorized the extension of the East Wing as long ago as 1905 but half a century passed before the funds were available and another five years before the job was done. In view of the current campaign to beautify the Capitol City as the showplace of the Nation, piloted by Mrs. Lyndon B. Johnson, they are hopeful, however, that action on the

West Wing can be accelerated and that the visitors of the future can climb its steps with pride, not fear, in the restoration of their national shrine.

INDEX

THE AUTHOR

TREVOR L. CHRISTIE, a professional writer for over thirty years, specializes in writing on international subjects of a cultural nature. Pursuit of this interest has taken him around the world several times. As a young newspaper reporter he spent a great deal of time in the Far East, and since then he has lived in Paris, Rome, Athens, and Beirut.

Mr. Christie's particular concern with antiquities and their preservation is one of long standing, and in the course of his travels he has visited most of the great monuments of both Western and Oriental civilization. A previous book by Mr. Christie, *Legacy of a Pharaoh*, dealt in detail with the Abu Simbel salvage operation. This writing project led almost inevitably to a book concerning similar situations all over the world, and so we have *Antiquities in Peril*.

When he is not journeying to the far reaches of the world, Mr. Christie lives in the Greenwich Village section of New York City.